Stocks are fun!

Part 1: Achieving financial freedom with dividends

Heikin Ashi Trader

DAO PRESS

Ormidia, Larnaca

An imprint of Splendid Island

TABLE OF CONTENTS

People learn to work for money, but they never learn to have money working for them.

Robert Kiyosaki

PART 1: IF IT IS NOT FUN, YOU WILL NOT HOLD OUT

1. Why stocks are fun

Stocks are fun, if only because they offer endless possibilities for making money. Most investors buy stocks in the hope that their market value will rise. Of course it is fun to watch how a stock, once you have bought it, increases in value over time. However, in this way, you turn stocks into objects of speculation.

Although there is not really anything wrong with this, it does not represent the main reason why people have bought stocks over the course of history. Earlier generations invested in stocks because they wanted to earn *a regular income* by owning them.

The companies rewarded these investors for their loyalty to their shares. This reward for the holding of shares eventually came to be referred to as a *dividend*. The word comes from the Latin "dividere", which means, "to share". This means that part of the profit is paid out in the form of dividends.

Many American, British and Canadian companies pay dividends four times a year. But did you know that some companies even pay out dividends every month? I have several such stocks in my portfolio. All I can say is that this is really fun. The company pays me a monthly dividend because I own some of their shares.

Isn't that incredible?

When I started trading stocks twenty years ago, I was only interested in price appreciation of stocks. I wanted to "earn" on shares by buying them at a certain price in the hope of selling them again at a higher price – for purely speculative purposes. I even did day trading with stocks. I bought stocks and sold them the same day. At a profit. And sometimes, at a loss. I am not ashamed to say that I sold at a loss more often than at a profit.

In those days, I did not even realize that there was another, much more relaxed way to make money with stocks. And that is exactly what this book is about. You will learn, step by step, how to find exactly those stocks. It will give you a well-thought-out method that, with time, will provide you with a regular income. This happens in a relaxed way, without you having to look at the daily ups and downs of the share prices.

On the contrary – you will see that it is much better (and much more fun) if you do *not* look at the price of your stocks every day. With our method, the current price is pretty much the least interesting thing there is. It is much more interesting and exciting when you can see what dividends your stocks pay out each month.

We want to stay calm and focus our attention on the income that our stocks generate for us, because this income (the dividends) is the fastest, most effective tool, with which you can one day replace the income you get from your regular work.

Yes, you heard right. The ultimate goal of an income investor is to, one day, have his income from dividends exceed the sum of his monthly expenses. This day is what some call their "Work Freedom Day" – the day when your dividend income has grown to such an extent that you no longer need to work.

If you look at the whole issue of money as a single game, you could say that was the day you won the game. You are the winner! That is the day when you are definitely financially free. You can either quit your job or not. Either way, it is very different from having to work for a living.

I can assure you that it is a lot of fun when the sum of your dividends enables you to make this decision.

In contrast to the speculator, who depends on the price development of his stocks, an income investor can lie back and relax, to a large extent, whether he actively takes care of his stocks or not. He can travel for months at a time, or simply disappear. And the dividends cheerfully continue to flow. They come in (from quarter to quarter, from year to year, even increasing inn value, as we will see further on in this book) – no matter whether the investor actively takes care of them, or does not look at his stock portfolio for months, or even years.

Even after your death, the dividends will continue to come in. I know of such a stock portfolio. It was set up by a married couple many years ago. After the couple had died, their children did not know what to do with it! There were plenty of five-figure dividends, and the portfolio had continued to grow, year after year.

With dividends, you can build up assets on the side. You can start small (and recently, even very small thanks to the disappearing fees!). You can start with USD 10. It does not matter. Dividend stocks hardly need any care or work. The money keeps flowing, whether you take care of it or not. Even when you die, the money continues to flow. If that is not fun, I don't know what is?

2. Why you should become an income investor

When it comes to money, most people are looking for security. They want the reassuring feeling of having a regular income. In most cases, this means that they accept a permanent job in order to achieve this goal. This job guarantees that they will never be "without money" for a month.

However, they pay a high price for this feeling of security. For one thing, of course, they have to show up every day. Their boss demands that they do their job day after day, year after year, whether they want to or not. If you enjoy your work, this is not a problem at first. When you are young and healthy, you are hungry for life and you want to experience being part of society. You want to "fit in." Maybe you have pleasant colleagues who mostly think the same way you do.

The problems start when you get older, or when your enthusiasm for the work you once loved dwindles. Suddenly you realize you are trapped. You have made yourself comfortable in a hamster wheel, but you are forced to keep running, so that the wheel keeps turning.

The hamster wheel is the way you once chose to trade your hours of life for money. Simply put, most people work for money. However, they have never seriously thought about what they could do with the money they earn (other than spending it).

Unlike this group (which sociologists refer to as "the small guy" or "the middle class"), the rich and wealthy do exactly the opposite. The wealthy do not work for money. Their money works for them. That is why they are wealthy and remain wealthy.

One might think that this is completely unfair.

But it is not simply unfair – it is much worse than that. Those who work for their money are also paying the highest taxes. It is the same in all developed countries. Those who slog and slave at a job every day pay the lion's share of the taxes.

On the other hand, it is a fact that wealthy people pay the least taxes. Firstly, they do not work for their money and secondly, they get their income from sources that demand low taxes, or no taxes at all.

Isn't that incredibly unfair?

It is not. It represents the high price that "employees" pay for the little bit of security that their job gives them. Employees are taxed the highest and often, they live from payday to payday. They have no choice but to work, earn money, work, earn money ad infinitum, until their retirement, which they really long for.

Money dominates their lives. They are slaves to money, although most of them would never see it that way. However, that's the way it is. The money problem has such a firm grip on these people that they think about it constantly.

Instead of working for money, the wealthy buy assets (or they create them, for example by starting a business). They buy or build assets that regularly put money in their pockets. Furthermore, the more money they have in their pockets, the more assets they buy.

When a wealthy person buys a house, it is usually not to live in (this is the dream of the middle class). They buy a house in order to generate an income from renting it to someone else. I know a man in Berlin who owns over seventy apartments. He can live like a prince on the rental income. However, he himself lives in a rented apartment. Think about it. This man has understood the game.

The same goes for companies owed by wealthy people, as well as for the stocks they buy. The difference between the rich and the poor also applies to stocks. The small guy (say, the middle class) buys stocks in the hope that they will rise. They bet on price appreciation. Wealthy people, on the other hand, buy stocks, the dividends of which will give them a steady income.

That is what this book is about. I want to talk about the stocks from which you can draw an income. I want to talk about the stocks that the wealthy buy, and not those that the middle class buys.

3. Why dividend income offers more security than your job

Today, I would go so far as to say that income from stocks is much safer than income from a job. Your job may be safe for now, but there are enough reasons to question the security of an employment relationship.

If you are in the private sector, your company could go bankrupt. A competitor could buy it, and your job could become redundant in the course of restructuring.

If you work for the state, your job is basically more secure. If you are a teacher or a civil servant, or if you have any other job that is guaranteed by the state, you might feel safe.

However, you should not forget that the biggest risk is not the state but *you*. As long as you are healthy and you can do your job, there is no problem. But, if you get sick or slip into burnout (I know a few people with this problem), things can suddenly look very different. In other words, whatever you do, however great your job might be, *you* are the biggest risk in terms of your income. You put all your eggs in one basket with this strategy: your job. May I say that from a financial point of view, this is a risky strategy. There is a lot that could go wrong in this situation.

It seems much safer to me, not to get your income from just from *one* source, but from dozens of sources. This is the goal of the income investor. Some dividend investors have fifty or even a hundred different stock positions that put money into their pockets every month. These people receive income from a hundred different sources. If one of them falls by the wayside, the investor hardly feels it (minus 1%). But if you lose the income from your job, you are going to feel it very sorely (minus 100%).

4. What you need most when you get older: A regular income!

As I am slowly approaching retirement age myself, I naturally know many people who are in this phase of their lives, or who have already retired. What strikes me particularly with the latter group, is that many of them have to make considerable cutbacks as soon as they retire. Most of them rely on Social Security. Although this is considered a guaranteed income, in many cases it is not enough – there is no way they can make ends meet.

The fact is that the cost of living does not decrease, as you get older. On the contrary, it often increases. For example, many people want to travel or spend money on their hobbies.

As long as you are still an employee, you might be able to cover the monthly costs, but once you have retired, your possibilities of earning extra money are limited. Besides that, what have you been working for all your life? Certainly not to go back to being an employee when you are old?

So the question becomes more urgent than ever: is the income from your Social Security going to be sufficient for you to live the lifestyle you have in mind?

When I raise the issue, I often get the answer: "My Social Security is enough. It is not very generous, but I get by". The problem is that many people have the nominal amount they will receive one day in mind. That is the figure the Social Security calculates for you, based on your years of employment. No matter how high this amount is, unfortunately it will never keep up with inflation (i.e. loss of purchasing power).

If you retire and get USD 1,391 a month in your first year (average monthly Social Security in 2017), after 20 years this USD 1,391 will be worth much less in terms of purchasing power. Of course, there will be adjustments, but they will not be sufficient to compensate for the real loss of purchasing power.

If you look at these figures, and are aware that most employees who rely on social insurance benefits have no additional protection at all, then you already know that our western countries are increasingly becoming a poorhouse. Those who have nevertheless saved a little extra over the years have usually invested it in annuities, the returns of which might also be unable to beat inflation.

On the other hand, studies have clearly shown, again and again, that stocks can maintain purchasing power the best, because they offer the highest returns in the end. They even increase purchasing power, which is certainly not the case in terms of insurances or bonds.

Of course, as a retired worker, you could get a job as a caretaker or a char. But, in my opinion, it would be better if you had a *second source of income* in addition to your pension.

By source of income, I do not mean a job. I mean real assets that put cash into your pocket every month, and that will even grow considerably from year to year. We refer to this as *passive income* (an income you do not have to work for).

A stock portfolio with dividend stocks best feeds such a source of income. Because even though you may no longer be involved in active working life, you indirectly remain a participant. As a shareholder of a company, you share in its profits. You receive regular payments in the form of dividends, so even as a retiree, you are still involved in economic life.

5. Why you need to understand the term „cash flow" if you want to become financially independent

The term cash flow indicates how healthy a company is in terms of its financial situation. The term cash flow simply means the money flow of a company. That is, what remains after you have deducted the expenses from the income of a company. If there is any cash flow at all, i.e. more income than expenses, we call it a *positive cash flow*. If there are more expenses than income, there is a *negative cash flow*.

The rich and wealthy buy stocks to ensure a regular cash flow, preferably one that will not dry up. For life. In this book, I will show you which stocks they choose to buy.

The wealthy, of course, focus on a positive cash flow. They want to generate a cash flow that far exceeds their expenses. Therefore, if you want to be financially independent yourself one day, it is important that you understand the term cash flow, because it will change your view of how you handle money fundamentally, just as it did with me when I stopped working for money.

I went to my boss at the time and put my letter of resignation down in front of him. He read it and looked at me with a mixture of amazement and disbelief. He could not believe that I was giving up such a good job.

For me, on the other hand, it felt like a liberation. I hated going to work every day, even if it was a great job with lots of freedom. I still did not feel free. You are only free when you no longer have a master. In that case, my master was not so much my boss, but the compulsion to go there every day, whether I wanted to or not.

Now, it is not at all necessary for you to quit your job tomorrow, as I did. On the contrary. It might even be an advantage for you to keep your job for now. Your job gives you the steady income you always need.

The idea of this book is to show you how you can gradually replace the income you get from working with the income you get from your assets. As soon as they begin to exceed your income from your employment, you are financially free.

This book is about stocks, but it is primarily about the financial freedom that the cash flow from your stocks will give you one day.

I owe a lot to the book "Rich Dad Poor Dad" by Robert Kiyosaki, whom I quoted at the beginning of the book. That book opened my eyes. It taught me to think about money the way the wealthy people of this world see money. Kiyosaki illustrates this with real estate investments, but the principle is the same for an equity investor, therefore I recommend this book.

I would like to develop a step by step a plan on how you can become financially independent with dividend stocks. That is why this book is not about speculating on the stock exchange. Whoever is interested in this can read my other books. This book is about how you can use the stock market in such a way that you can earn *an income* from it, just as you earn an income from your job. The subtle difference is that you do not have to work for this second income.

Therefore, I prefer to talk about *income investing* or *cash flow investing*, because that is exactly what it is.

As you might know, there are other ways to achieve this. You could buy real estate and rent it out, as Kiyosaki recommends. On the other hand, you could also start a business.

These three ways – income investing with stocks, owning real estate or starting a business – are the three most effective ways to become financially independent. If you look at the Forbes list of the wealthiest people on the planet, you will discover that they have all chosen one of these three ways. The way you choose is up to you, and it only depends on your qualifications and your preferences.

Personally, I am not a fan of real estate. However, I know people like my friend in Berlin, with his seventy apartments, who are very successful with it.

I would never claim that any one of these methods is better or worse. All three have their advantages and disadvantages, as well as their special requirements.

It is a well-known fact that you need capital to buy property – a whole lot of capital. Of course, there are various ways you could get it, but that would be the subject of another book.

Starting a business is easier said than done. You might be successful with such a venture, but there are no guarantees. However, it is highly probable that you will fail with your first business, as happened in my case.

Buying dividend stocks in order to earn an income from them, on the other hand, is a viable path that many have taken before you. In my eyes, it is the easiest way. With some preparation and a little bit of knowledge, it will almost certainly lead you to your goal.

The discipline and staying power needed to build a successful company is similar to that required if you want to become financially independent with dividend stocks. Therefore, you should never underestimate what it takes. The main difficulty is not that you do not understand the principle of dividend investing. The challenge is to execute this strategy in a disciplined manner, month after month, and year after year.

The difference between income investing and building a business is that you can fail with a business. With dividend stocks, on the other hand, it is almost impossible to fail if you follow a few principles. That is why I believe that, for most people, income investing with dividends is the way to go.

With stocks, it is possible to see the first cash flow in your account after just a few months. I can tell you from my own experience that this is a lot of fun. It is fun just watching how you are paid, month after month, simply for owning shares in a particular company. Moreover, it is fun to watch how this flow of money gradually begins to grow, and never dries up again. I will describe how to do this in the next chapters.

6. Why your bank advisor does not recommend that you become an income investor

Why have you hardly heard anything about income investing or cash flow investing so far? The reason is very simple: Neither banks, nor brokers, nor any other "advisors" make any money on income investors.

An income investor buys shares with the aim of keeping them "forever". Of course, there are some exceptions (we will take a look at them in another chapter). Usually, you buy your shares once, and that is it. In other words, there are no further commissions or annual fees or whatever else the stock exchange industry may think up. All the money that is distributed goes to you. The "advisors" get nothing. Why would the stock exchange industry advertise this kind of investment?

You can be sure that, if you tell your bank advisor about your new idea, he will point out the "risks". He will do his best to get the idea out of your mind. So be prepared! If not, so much the better. But keep in mind that the stock market industry (which earns a lot from the fees charged) will not provide any information in this regard. Hardly any glossy brochures on the subject of income investing are intended to give you a feeling of solidity or security. You will not see many TV shows or interviews with experts on the matter.

In other words, you are alone with your idea.

Well, not quite. On the internet, you will find communities that support you with tips and advice. If you need some kind of confirmation that what you are doing is right, you will have to get it from there. There are dozens of dividend bloggers, some of whom are celebrated as real superstars. You can usually only find them on the internet (see Addendum).

Of course, I recommend that you always use your own brains when making purchasing decisions, and not just buy what Blogger XYZ recommends. However, I can say that some of these dividend bloggers write with great expertise. If you have been doing this for years, there is a good chance that you will become an expert in this field.

7. As an income investor, you are (and will remain) involved in economic life

There is another reason why I recommend dealing with and owning stocks. If you have stocks in a company, you become a co-owner of that company. You may only own a very small share, but this will awaken within you an interest in the business of that company. And, the more shares you have in that company, the more interested you will become.

The more different stocks you have in your portfolio, the more you will broaden your horizon. Suddenly you will become interested in drugstore distribution chains, oil pipelines and liquid gas. You will start to read about commercial real estate, about the pension liabilities of a car company. The knowledge you acquire here is not abstract. It is in your best interest that the companies and the industries you have invested in thrive and prosper. Dividends are paid out of a company's cash flow, which means that it comes mainly from the profits it generates from its business. If the profit disappears, the dividend is in danger, and this will eventually affect your own cash flow.

I am always amazed at how little some people know about the industries they have nothing to do with in their jobs.

However, is that true? Isn't it true that in the end, everything is connected to everything else? Isn't it true that some contracts with utilities companies determine the amount of your gas bill? Isn't it so that the ups and downs of the US economy determine how many jobs are created?

The more stocks you have, the more insight you will gain into how everything is interwoven with everything else. You cannot just walk away from this and say "I don't care". You may find that many things in the economy are in trouble and should be different. Well, if you invest in stocks, you have a chance to get actively involved, by making your own choice regarding what you want to invest in and what you do not want to invest in. By doing so, you play a role in changing the economy.

When you start to receive dividends from different sectors of the economy, it all becomes much more concrete. As a shareholder, you are paid for holding shares in these companies. This means nothing less than that you provide these companies with *your own money* so that they can operate or perhaps even expand. This creates a mutual relationship that you can shape yourself. Furthermore, at some point, this relationship will enable you to become financially independent.

PART 2: INTRODUCTION TO THE WORLD OF DIVIDENDS

1. What are dividends?

A dividend is the distribution of profits by a company to its shareholders. The term dividend comes from the Latin word "dividere", which means "to distribute". Therefore, it is a fixed amount that is "distributed" among shareholders, when the company has made a profit.

Historically, the Dutch East India Company (VOC) was the first company that ever paid regular dividends. Those who held shares in the VOC were lucky, because during its almost 200-year existence (1602-1800) the VOC paid annual dividends worth around 18 percent of the share value.

Each shareholder receives a cash payment for each of the shares he or she holds. If a company decides to pay a dividend of USD two and a shareholder has 100 shares, he or she receives a dividend of USD 200. If someone holds 1,000 shares, they will receive a dividend of USD 2,000.

It is important to note that investors receive the dividend regardless of the development of the share price. Good payers of dividends are even in a position to pay the dividend in "times of crisis." For example, this was the case during the financial crisis of 2007-2008. Those who held shares of the typical dividend payers at that time, such as Coca Cola, Procter & Gamble, Walmart or Johnson & Johnson, received their dividends, even though share prices plummeted.

Dividend payments thus made up for at least part of the losses in terms of price. Incidentally, the shares of good dividend payers recovered rapidly after the crisis. Studies have shown that the share price of reliable dividend payers generally returned to pre-crisis levels faster than other shares. This is reason enough to have a closer look at these robust stocks.

2. Why do companies pay dividends?

When a company makes a profit, it has two options. It can retain the profit and invest in current or future business. Alternatively, it can distribute part of the profits to its shareholders.

A company pays dividends from its profits because it wants to reward its shareholders for putting their capital at its disposal.

However, paying a dividend is not a legal obligation. Companies such as Facebook or Amazon, for example, do not currently pay dividends (as of March 2020). In contrast, Apple started paying dividends in 2012.

In general, companies that are still in a growth phase tend not to pay dividends. They invest their profits in further growth, instead of distributing them to shareholders. Amazon is known for investing in more and more business areas, in order to grow even further, despite huge earnings.

More mature companies, such as McDonalds, IBM and Microsoft, pay dividends to their shareholders. The reason is simple. A good dividend attracts investors, especially *income investors*, who may remain loyal to their shares for decades.

Besides, you would not act any differently if you were the owner of a company yourself. If your company made a profit, you would probably pay yourself a cash dividend. Maybe you would reinvest the profits in the company in the beginning, to make it grow faster. However, at some point you would want to see the fruits of your labor.

There is another reason why companies pay dividends. Dividends ensure that the management of a company is "financially disciplined". Thus, it becomes less likely that the company will use money to finance projects that may eventually turn out to be a failure. Studies prove that, over long periods, dividend shares perform better than non-dividend shares.

3. When do companies pay dividends?

If you invest in US dividend stocks, there are a few dates to consider. First, it must be clear who, among the shareholders, has the right to receive dividends. The *dividend record date* is the day on which it is determined which shareholders are eligible to receive a dividend. You must have the stock in your portfolio before this record date if you want to receive the dividend.

However, watch out! It is not the record date that counts, but rather the e*x-dividend date.* The ex-dividend *date* is set exactly one business day before the dividend record date. Therefore, if you want to benefit from the dividend, you must have the stock in your portfolio before the ex-dividend date, i.e. at least two days before the record date.

Then there is the *Dividend Date*. This is the day on which the dividend is actually paid out.

Now, you might be asking yourself why it is regulated this way; there are good reasons for it. Some investors buy the stock before the record date, collect the dividend and then sell it again afterwards. I do not consider this to be a clever strategy. On the dividend day, the share price usually falls by an amount roughly equal to the dividend paid. This is logical, since on that day, the shareholders are a bit "richer", but the company is "poorer", because it has distributed part of the company's assets as dividends.

That is why there is a "discount" on that particular share. Dividend hunters are therefore at a disadvantage because they lose as much as they have gained. They also have to pay commissions for buying and selling the share. But, for long-term investors, the dividend discount is no problem. If you study long term price charts, you will hardly notice the effects of this discount.

4. What is the dividend yield?

The dividend yield tells an investor what return he can expect when buying a stock. The dividend yield is the ratio between the annual dividend payment amount of a share and its current price. Since the price of a share changes constantly, the dividend yield naturally changes with it. The dividend yield increases if the share price falls, because the buyer pays less money for the same number of shares. This is also the reason why real dividend hunters are actually "happy" when share prices "decrease", as this enables them to improve their positions at lower prices (i.e. buy more shares) and thus receive a higher yield.

If the price of a share rises, the dividend yield also falls automatically. An investor must now dig deeper into his pockets to buy the same number of shares. If a company's share price rises constantly, it will have to increase its dividend payout if it wants to maintain its dividend yield.

To calculate the dividend yield, one must divide the annual dividends by the current share price.

Dividend yield = annual dividend/share price

If the price of a particular share is USD 100 and the company pays a dividend of USD 3, the dividend yield on that share is 3%.

USD 3 / USD 100 = 0.03

The 0.03 expressed as a percentage gives a return of 3%.

If the share price rises to USD 120 and the company does not increase the dividend payment, the return falls to 0.025 or 2.5%.

It is important to emphasize that the dividend yield is calculated based on the *annual return*. In other words, it is not calculated based on quarterly, semi-annual or monthly payments.

5. What is the payout ratio?

The dividend payout ratio is the ratio of the total value of the dividends paid to shareholders, to the net profit of the company. It is the percentage of profit that a company distributes to its shareholders as dividends. The company retains the amount that is not paid out to their shareholders. The company may need it to pay off debt, reinvest in its core business, or increase cash reserves.

Some companies distribute almost all their profits to shareholders. At the same time, many companies pay out only part of their profits and some pay out nothing at all. The internet giant Amazon is a good example. Although Amazon makes huge profits, it is still in a growth phase. It spends huge sums of money to grow its income and expand its business. Profit margins are razor-thin during this growth period. Nevertheless, the company has been profitable for the last ten years, except in 2014. There is a good chance that Amazon will begin to pay dividends one day, if growth slows down and cash flow continues to grow.

Paying a dividend usually means that a company has left its growth phase behind. The payout ratio often depends on the degree of maturity of the company. Apple (AAPL), for example, started paying a dividend in 2012. Management had difficulties in justifying the company's huge cash flow with a payout ratio of 0%.

A low payout ratio is usually an indication that the company has sufficient income to guarantee future dividend payments. It can use the cash reserves to increase the dividend year after year. Investors who are looking for dividend growth naturally prefer those companies.

A high payout ratio (over 80%, for example) is a sign that the company is paying out most of its profits as dividends. The danger here is that the company could be forced to stop increasing the dividend, or even reduce it, if any financial difficulties arise (this was the case during the Corona crisis). In the worst case, it could be forced to stop paying out dividends altogether. Therefore, a high payout ratio is a warning sign.

In general, a payout ratio of about 30 to 50% indicates that the company has sustainable reserves to further increase the dividend. At the same time, it still has sufficient funds to support its business activities. If you have a savings period of 20 years or more ahead of you, you should give preference to investing in such companies.

However, there are exceptions, where even very high payout ratios are perfectly justifiable. One example was the Coca-Cola stock in early 2020, which had a payout ratio of 88%. However, it was far below the five-year average of 175 %. Despite the high payout ratio, the company has increased its annual dividend payout for the past 57 consecutive years.

Some companies distribute even more than 100% of their profits to shareholders. Procter & Gamble had a payout ratio of 188% in early 2020, which was due to a one-time distribution of assets, in addition to earnings. Therefore, you should pay close attention if you think the payout ratio is too high. In the case of Procter & Gamble, it is important to remember that the company has paid a dividend since 1891 and has increased its annual payout for the last 66 consecutive years.

6. Why should you invest in dividend stocks?

Investing in high-dividend quality stocks is an excellent way to build wealth over time. When I first heard about dividends, I did not think it was worth looking into. "What is the point of 3% a year? " I thought. Unfortunately, I had never considered *the compound interest effect* that such an investment entails. Nor had I ever heard of *dividend growth*. To me, it seemed like something for people with large assets. I thought that if I had little money, I would have to do things quite differently on the stock market to become wealthy. It took me quite a while to realize my mistake.

If you systematically reinvest the dividends (by buying more shares with the dividends, which in turn pay more dividends), you are building up a money machine that will eventually run on its own. It is a relatively safe method for building wealth, that has been proven a thousand times. To demonstrate the power of dividend stocks, let us look at some examples of ordinary people who have become wealthy, thanks to dividend stocks.

7. Ordinary people who became millionaires, thanks to dividends

Example 1: Anne Scheiber

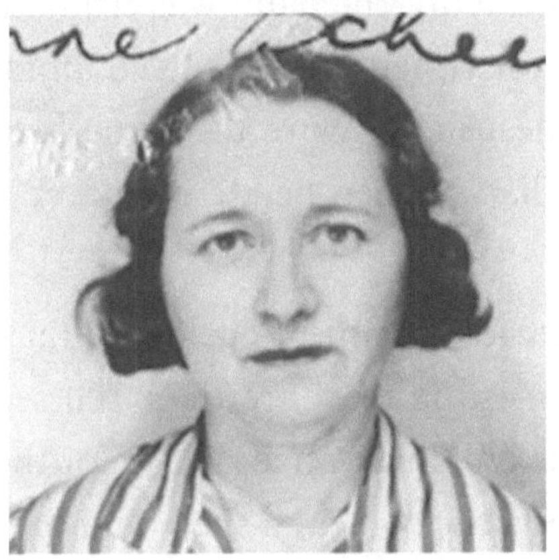

In 1935, Anne Scheiber, who was of Jewish origin, worked as an accountant for the tax office in the US state of Tennessee. She earned a salary of USD 3,150 per annum. Since she had no children and lived modestly, she managed to save USD 5,000, which she began to invest in stocks. Anne Scheiber never received a salary of more than USD 4,000 per annum and had never been promoted.

In 1944, Anne Scheiber retired at the age of fifty-one. Her stock portfolio had already grown to a value of

USD 21,000 by that time. (Adjusted for inflation this would be about USD 297,000 today).

She moved into a small apartment in Manhattan, near Central Park. She drew an annual pension of USD 3,100 but continued to deal on the stock market for the next fifty years. Although her fortune continued to grow from year to year, she maintained her modest lifestyle. Reportedly, the paint was crumbling from the walls of her apartment and she lived amidst dusty old furniture. She usually wore the same black coat and a matronly hat on her head, whenever she left her apartment.

Over the decades, Anne Scheiber built up a stock portfolio consisting of more than 100 securities. She did not focus on "innovative stocks" or the high-flyers of the time. On the contrary, she bought the blue chips, i.e. stocks that have long since passed their growth phase. These are the companies whose prices have long since stopped rising sharply. For example, she bought stocks of the beverage producers Coca-Cola and Pepsi. She had shares in the Paramount film studio and large pharmaceutical companies such as Schering-Plough (now Merck & Co).

Although she had long been wealthy, she maintained her thrifty and somewhat eccentric lifestyle. According to an anecdote, she took home the food from a shareholders' meeting she attended, in order to eat feed herself for the next three days. Until her death in 1995, she lived in the same apartment and wore the same clothes as in 1944.

Anne Scheiber was, as it were, the epitome of the thrifty income investor. She ignored all price fluctuations on the stock market and consistently reinvested the dividends. She never sold a share, not even when the stock market was falling sharply, as during the economic crisis in the early 1970s or during the "Black Monday" crash in 1987.

At the time of her death, 30 percent of her portfolio consisted of bonds, because in the last years of her life, Scheiber used the dividends to buy tax-free municipal bonds. At the end of her life, the value of her portfolio was around USD 22 million. The dividends alone totaled around USD 750,000 per year.

Scheiber bequeathed her entire fortune to the private Jewish Yeshiva University in New York. Nobody at the university had ever heard of her. Incidentally, this institution also produced some other well-known personalities, such as the authors Herman Wouk and Chaim Potok, as well as the neurologist Oliver Sacks.

Now, let's have a look at the top ten positions in Anne Scheiber's portfolio at the time of her death.

Figure 1: Anne Scheiber's equity portfolio, largest positions in 1995

Company	Shares owned	$ Price 1995	value	Gain
Schering-Plough (SGP)	64,000	59.25	3,788,800	62%
Pepsico (Pep)	27,000	57.5	1,552,500	65%
Allied Signal (ald)	20,934	49.25	1,030,999	44%
Loews (LTR)	14,061	78	1,096,758	75%
Bristol-Myers Squibb (BMY)	10,080	84.5	851,760	45%
Coca-Cola (KO)	9,048	79.25	717,054	60%
Allegheny Power System (AYP)	8,000	28.25	226,000	30%
Rockwell International (ROK)	4,640	51.75	240,120	46%
Unocal (UCL)	3690	28.75	106,087	10%
Exxon (Xon)	1664	84	139,776	39%
Total	163,117		9,749,854	

Anne Scheiber built up significant positions in the pharmaceutical companies Schering-Plough and Bristol-Myers Squibb. This is not untypical for dividend portfolios. Pharmaceutical companies are mostly good dividend payers. In Schering-Plough, Anne Scheiber built up a huge position of 64,000 shares over the decades! At the time of her death, this position alone corresponded to a fortune of USD 3,788,800.

She also had large stock positions in PepsiCo and Coca-Cola. No wonder, since both companies are also robust dividend payers. We also find the typical utilities, like the Allegheny Power System of Pennsylvania. With shares in Unocal (acquired by Chevron in 2005) and Exxon, she also had oil and gas in her portfolio.

All of these equity companies are traditional – one could almost say "boring" – dividend classics. It also made sense for Anne Scheiber to build up long-term equity positions in these companies, because the probability that they would go bust was very low. Rather, they were bought by a competitor, as was the case with Schering-Plough, Allied, Rockwell International and Unocal. Investors do not need to fear takeovers. On the contrary, they usually go hand in hand with sharply rising share prices, which flushes additional money into the dividend investor's portfolio.

Example 2: Ronald Read

Our second investor, like Anne Scheiber, has an incredible history and, thus, fits into the category of "hidden millionaires". Read was the type of person who few would have suspected was rich. He grew up in Dummerston, Vermont, in an impoverished farming community. He walked or 6.4 km a day, or hitched a ride, to his high school, and was the first high school graduate in his family. In World War II, he enlisted in the army and served as a military policeman in Italy. After the war, Read returned to Brattleboro, Vermont, and worked as a gas station attendant and mechanic for about 25 years. For one year, Read "retired", then he took on a job as a janitor for the next seventeen years, until 1997.

Read is said to have loved chopping wood. He often drove his car to his family's homestead to collect firewood. He also picked up branches from the ground for his wood stove.

Read collected stamps and coins. He regularly drank coffee at the Brattleboro Memorial Hospital café, and he always ate an English muffin with peanut butter for breakfast. The hospital's development manager got him his first library card in 2007. After that, he visited the library regularly, and always went home with a stack of books.

When he died in 2014, he bequeathed USD 1.2 million to Brooks Memorial Library and USD 4.8 million to Brattleboro Memorial Hospital. It turned out that Read had a dividend portfolio worth nearly USD eight million.

Read, too, had only invested in blue chip stocks. He avoided technology companies. For decades, he also patiently reinvested the dividends he received. For that reason, we will also look at Read's ten most important positions.

Figure 2: Ronald Read ten top equity positions

Company	value in $
Wells Fargo	510,900
Procter & Gamble	364008
Colgate-Palmolive	252104
American Express	199034
J.M. Smucker	189722
Johnson & Johnson	183881
VF Corp.	152208
McCormick	145055
Raytheon	142970
United Technologies	140880
Total	**2,280,762**

As we can see, Ronald Read's ten "largest" positions formed only the smaller part of his overall portfolio. We do not know his other positions, but it is reasonable to assume that Read had a diversified portfolio made up of dozens of companies. Nevertheless, it is interesting to see which companies Read invested the most money in.

His largest position was Wells Fargo, a bank with a market capitalization of USD 274 billion (2017). It is the second most valuable bank in the world, after JP Morgan Chase. Berkshire Hathaway, the company owned by Warren Buffet, currently holds 9.8% of the shares. In second and third place, we have Procter & Gamble (Gillette, Always, Oil of Olay, Oral-B, and Pampers) and Colgate Palmolive (Ajax, Elmex, and Aronal), two consumer goods companies. It could hardly be more "boring"...

American Express hardly needs any introduction. J.M. Smucker is a producer of jam, peanut butter and ice cream. VF Corp is a clothing company (Lee Jeans, Wrangler). With Johnson & Johnson, Read also invested some money in a pharmaceutical company. McCormick is a tractor manufacturer. With Raytheon (Patriot), Read also had shares in an armaments company and with United Technologies, he brought a technology company on board – one that is active in space travel, but which also builds elevator systems and air conditioning.

If you look at Read's list, something else stands out too. Almost all the companies are over 100 years old.

Wells Fargo 1852

Procter & Gamble 1837

Colgate Palmolive 1806

J.M. Smucker 1897

Johnson & Johnson 1886

VFCorp 1899

McCormick 1856

Only Raytheon (1927) and United Technologies (Steel Propeller was the predecessor in 1919) are somewhat "younger". In other words, Read did not build his fortune with modern technology companies. He relied almost entirely on the dinosaurs of the industrial age. All these companies have a long history of dividends and are part of the backbone of the American economy. Read was just the classic example of an investor who bets on high-quality blue chip stocks and patiently reinvests the dividends paid by these giants over decades!

Example 3: Grace Groner

There is probably no story that illustrates the power of the dividend strategy better than that of Grace Groner.

She was born in 1909, in a small farming community in Lake County, Illinois. At the age of twelve, she and her twin sister, Gladys became orphans. The two girls were taken in by one of the members of the community, George Anderson. He financed Grace's studies at nearby Lake Forest College. The Anderson family simply regarded her as part of the family. Grace lived with Ann Findlay, an older relative, in a small one bedroomed cottage. She never married and worked as a secretary for Abbott Laboratories for 43 years. She had few needs and never owned a car in her life. She bought her clothes at jumble sales and, apparently, she always gave money to those in need. The only luxury she afforded herself, was traveling.

In 1935, Groner invested USD 180 in three shares of Abbott Laboratories, the company she worked for. She then reinvested the dividends for the next 75 years. She never sold a single share. Her Abbott stock was split several times over the next 75 years. Grace Groner did nothing more than reinvest Abbot dividends in new Abbot Shares, year after year. It was the only company she ever bought shares in. By the end of her life, she had over 100,000 Abbott shares.

No one knew that the unremarkable senior citizen had amassed a fortune. After her death in 2010, her estate totaled more than USD seven million. It was bequeathed to a foundation she had established before her death. It is estimated that the foundation received USD 300,000 annually, in interest from her estate. She expressed the wish that the money go to the students of Lake Forest College. The money was used to finance independent studies, internships, international study and service projects, as well as a scholarship for students of the pharmaceutical school. The head of the School Foundation "almost fell off his chair" when he heard about Grace Groner's donation to the school.

We do not need to study Grace Groner's "stock portfolio" any further, because it consisted of shares in just one company: Abbott Laboratories, the company where she had worked as a secretary for 43 years.

With an "initial investment" of USD 180, with which she could buy just three shares, she built up a fortune of more than USD seven million over decades. Mind you: with stocks from a single company!

Abbot Laboratories was founded in Abbott Park, North Chicago, Illinois in 1888. The core business of the pharmaceutical company, which has around 73,000 employees, is the research, development and production of various drugs for human and veterinary medicine, as well as work in the fields of laboratory diagnostics and clinical nutrition. The company is one of the *dividend aristocrats*, a group of dividend shares with more than 25 years of consecutive dividend increases.

8. What is the compound interest effect?

The three examples beautifully demonstrate that anyone who wants to build up assets over the long term, should consider the "compound interest effect". This "effect", which Albert Einstein also called "the eighth wonder of the world", is the decisive difference between being one of the winners or one of the losers of the money game, one day. It may sound a little cruel, but the fact is that understanding this effect determines whether you will have to work for money all your life, or whether money will start working for you one day.

To understand the compound interest effect, we must first understand simple interest. Everybody is familiar with the concept. Imagine you have USD 1,000 and you find an investment that gives you 10% per year. In this case, after one year your money will earn you 10% or USD 100. After one year, you will have capital of USD 1,100.

Unfortunately, most people do not appreciate this 10% return. They say to themselves: "We will spend the USD 100 on a good meal." Nothing wrong with that! In a year's time, you can go out to dinner again, because the capital will have earned another 10%, and there will be USD 1,100 in your account again. One could almost make a nice tradition out of this annual meal.

However, there is a problem with simple interest. It does not allow your capital to grow. It remains at USD 1,000. In fact, it is even worse than that – due to annual inflation, your USD 1,000 loses purchasing power with each passing year. If you were able to eat at a good restaurant with your USD 100 in the first year, in ten years you will probably only be able to afford a pizza stand. USD 100 today by no means has the same value as USD 100 in ten years.

Now, we come to compound interest. Instead of having dinner every year, you leave the annual interest in the account. That way, instead of consuming it, you reinvest your USD 100. After two years, not only will your starting capital have grown, but the 10% interest you reinvested will also have earned interest.

After the second year, your capital is : USD 1,100 x 1,10 = USD 1,210

You have now received two times USD 100 in interest, plus USD 10 in *compound interest*. This USD 10 is the first compound interest you receive from your investment. Instead of USD 100 (as in the first year), our investment has now earned USD 110. A slightly better restaurant, if you like.

At first glance, this still looks modest, but let us take a closer look at what happens if we let this compound interest, together with our simple interest, continue to "work" for us.

After five years, we get earn USD 146.41 in interest, and our capital has grown to USD 1,610.51.

After ten years, we receive USD 235.80 in interest. Our capital has now grown to USD 2,593.75. The restaurants are getting really good...

After twenty years, our capital is generating USD 611.59. The capital counter now stands at USD 6,727.52!

After thirty years, finally our investment distributes USD 1,586.31annually, which is more than the original stake of USD 1,000! We now have a total capital of USD 17,449.44. This means that our initial stake has increased seventeen-fold! I hope that this demonstrates the power of compound interest to the reader. At this point, our money has long since started "working" for us.

Incidentally, after 50 years, we would have earned USD 117,391 – with a one-off investment of just USD 1,000! Over the years, we have not added a single cent to the initial capital. Graphically, the growth looks like this:

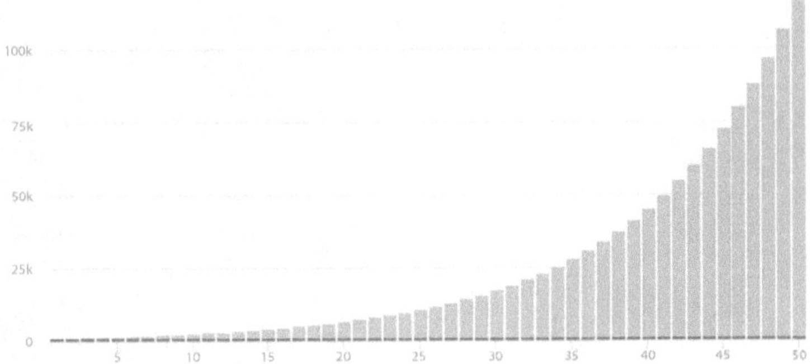

The small dark blue bar from the start (left on the graph) represents our initial capital of USD 1000. The light blue bar above this is the interest it makes. As you may see, the growth of our USD 1,000 investment is rather slow at the beginning, however, after 15 to 20 years, it really picks up speed. Our capital begins to grow more and more, thanks to the compound interest effect. This means that the curve begins to grow "exponentially". It does not only grow because the interest rate makes the capital grow year by year. It also grows because the *interest rate itself* begins to grow. If you look at it backwards, the jumps get bigger and bigger, as you can see in the diagram.

Most people are likely to know this effect under the term "snowball system". The so-called "chain letter" is a good example. If someone receives a chain letter and forwards it to ten other people, who in turn forward it to ten people each, then, theoretically, 100,000 letters have already been sent after the fifth recipient. Moreover, since the Corona crisis, everyone knows what an *exponential curve* means.

9. Which is better: high dividends or dividend growth?

When talking about dividends, beginners are often enthusiastic about companies that pay "high" dividends. These companies do, of course, exist. Dividends of eight, nine, or even more than ten percent seem to be the solution to earn at least "some" return on your money, because interest, in the true sense of the word, hardly exists anymore.

Worse. We have long since entered the age of *negative interest rates*. In plain language: if you leave your money in your savings account, you may have less money after one year, than in the year before. Monetary depreciation or inflation (better: real purchasing power of money) are not yet taken into account. So, a dividend of nine percent is very welcome as an alternative, isn't it? Because then you at least get something out of your money and you maintain your purchasing power.

As plausible as this idea seems to be, it unfortunately often leads to incorrect conclusions. It is precisely the effects of the low interest rate environment that have led to many companies paying high dividends, but this also results in their having excessive debt. You might, temporarily, have a well-paying dividend share in your portfolio, but it could turn out to be a ticking time bomb.

Instead of focusing exclusively on the highest yielding stocks, the experienced dividend investor tends to focus on companies with an established history of dividend growth. Companies with decades of consistent dividend payments are generally more reliable than high dividend payers. Therefore, someone with experience is more likely to build his portfolio with shares of companies that pay sustainable and, above all, *growing* dividends. Studies have shown that such a portfolio is more robust because it offers protection against market fluctuations and slower economic growth.

Dividends are paid out of a company's profits and are independent of the current market price of the share. If a company has been paying a dividend reliably for decades (without cutting it), it is a much better indicator of corporate performance than the interest level.

A high dividend is often the expression of a sharp decline in the stock price. If the price was USD 100 and the company paid a dividend of USD 3, the dividend yield was just 3%. If the share price now falls to USD 30 and the company keeps its shareholders calm by continuing to pay a dividend of USD 3 a year, the current yield, in relation to the share price, becomes 10%. This may make a yield hunter's mouth water, but it does not hide the fact that the share price has fallen to less than a third of the prior value.

This is why experienced dividend investors tend to look at the regular increase of the dividend. If a company increases its dividend every year, it means that the interest on the shares I buy today will be much higher next year. Therefore, with each year that I retain my investment in this company, the percentage value of my dividend, in relation to my initial investment, will increase.

Let us take a hypothetical stock as an example – one which is currently trading at exactly USD 100 in the market. If the company pays a dividend of USD 3 today, the return on my capital is 3%. If the company increases its dividend to USD3.30 the following year, the return on my capital increases to 3.30%. Although this increase may seem "insignificant" at first sight, this increase in the dividend represents an increase of 10%.

If an income investor relies mainly on stocks with a dividend that increases annually, he or she is betting on a steadily increasing return on his capital. Most investors who rely on dividend growth aim for dividend distributions that increase by between 5% and 10% or more annually.

One well-known example is Coca Cola. This company has been increasing its dividend for 57 years. Although growth has slowed somewhat in recent years (March 2020), the dividend has still grown by 6.91% over the last ten years! Coca Cola is a real cash machine that simply makes its investors happy.

However, there is another aspect of dividend growth that answers the question of whether you should bet on dividend growth or rather on a high dividend: *accumulated dividends*. The best way to look at this is to look at an example. Let us assume that we have a choice between a stock with a lower dividend and a high dividend growth, and a stock with a high dividend without dividend growth.

Share 1: dividend yield of 3.3 %

       dividend growth 10 %

Share 2: dividend yield of 7.5 %

       dividend growth 0 %

Figure 4: Dividend yield against dividend growth

(Comparison of Annual Dividends)   (Comparison of Cumulative Dividends)

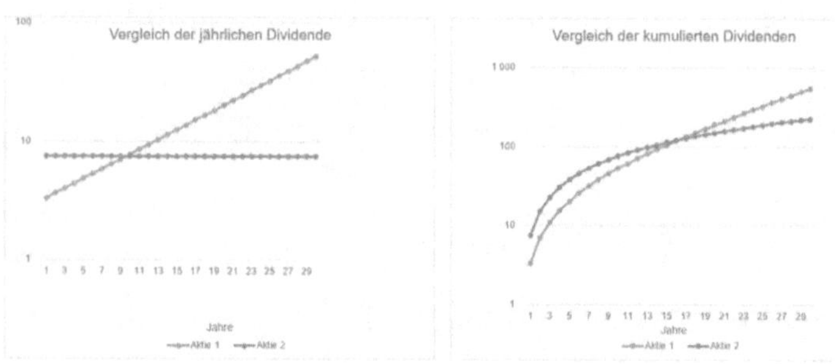

The red line symbolizes Share 1 and the blue line, Share 2. In the chart on the left, we see that, as expected, Share 2 generates significantly higher returns than Share 1 in the first ten years. It takes eleven years for Share 1 to catch up with Share 2, but then it begins to generate significantly higher returns.

However, if we look at the right-hand chart, a completely different picture emerges. The chart graphically demonstrates the *cumulative dividends*, i.e. the sum of all dividends paid out for both shares. If we look at this aspect, we see that the investor had to wait 17 years before Share 1 generated a cumulative higher return than Share 2. Moreover, it took almost 30 years for the difference to become significant.

This fact naturally raises questions about how much time an investor has for his or her investment. Those who have a lot of time (and are young) should therefore rather focus on dividend growth. Investors whose investment period is limited to ten years, or to a maximum of 20 years (investors in their forties or fifties), should therefore concentrate on investing their portfolio in shares that generate a higher return.

Examples of shares with higher dividends today (March 2020) are Altria (8.5%) or AT&T (6.4%), i.e. shares with a dividend yield of over 5%. If you are younger, you can easily add shares that have *more growth potential,* and therefore pay lower dividends now, to your portfolio. Candidates in February 2020 would be Apple (1.3 %), eBay (1.9 %) or Starbucks (2.6 %). Although the dividend yields of these companies are low now, they are all companies that generate high profits and could easily increase their dividends for years to come.

10. Which sectors pay the highest dividends?

If you start to go a little deeper into the subject of dividends, you will soon find that there are sectors that pay significantly higher dividends than others do. Technology companies, for example, generally do not pay lavish dividends. The reason is simple. Many technology companies are growth companies. They tend to reinvest profits, in order to grow faster.

Telecommunication companies, utilities and insurers are more often established companies, with customers who have to pay bills or insurance premiums on a regular basis. This provides these companies with a reliable cash flow, therefore they are able to pay out higher dividends to their shareholders.

Here, I will list the most important sectors of the US economy and mention some of the best-known dividend payers. The dividend yield dates from March 2020 (i.e. during the Corona crisis). Therefore, it is a snapshot. It is only intended to give the reader some orientation. Please note that the dividend yield can change at any time, due to share price changes.

The **technology sector** covers several industries, including telecommunications, IT services, semiconductor manufacturing, software and data hosting services, biotechnology and scientific research. There are many well-known names in this sector, such as Alphabet (Google), Facebook and Microsoft. The dividend yield of technology companies is generally low.

Good and well-known dividend payers are IBM (5.07 %), Cisco (3.63 %), Verizon (4.33 %) and AT&T (5.62 %).

The **Basic Materials sector** consists of several components, including oil and gas, metals, chemicals, construction materials, forestry, wood and paper products.

Good dividend payers here are Exxon Mobil (7.3%), Chevron (5.41%) and Dow Inc. (7.19%).

Consumer goods are products that are not bought by manufacturers and companies, but by consumers. Here, we find car parts, food, paper products and clothing. The consumer goods sector is usually divided into two categories: cyclical and non-cyclical. Cyclical consumer goods include products and services for consumer transport, including airlines, entertainment, restaurants and toys. Non-cyclical goods include products that are typically less affected by the business cycle. Such goods include food, beverages and tobacco.

Good dividend payers in this sector include Coca Cola (2.97%), Procter & Gamble (2.45%), Colgate Palmolive (2.37%) and Altria (7.4%).

The **financial sector** is comprised of several money-related industries, including banking, savings and loans, insurance and real estate. Although the sector generated attractive returns in the past, it was hard hit by the financial crisis of 2008-2009.

Regular dividend payers here include Bank of America (2.8%) and JPMorgan Chase (3.33%).

The **healthcare sector** is made up of companies that are active in biotechnology, pharmaceuticals, healthcare services, medical products, medical devices and accessories. In this sector, there are seven companies whose dividends have increased for 25 consecutive years, including Johnson & Johnson (2.68%), Merck (2.97%) and Pfizer (4.34%).

The **industrial goods sector** comprises companies that manufacture industrial products or provide services.

Although the average dividend yield in this sector is low, it includes some good dividend payers: Caterpillar (3.39 %), 3M (3.83 %) and Honeywell (2.19 %).

The **services sector** includes companies that produce or sell intangible goods, wholesalers and freight forwarding companies. This sector includes business services, restaurants, food shops and accommodation.

Good dividend payers here include The Home Depot (2.63 %), McDonalds (2.51 %) and Starbucks (2.18 %).

The **utilities sector** is divided into electricity, gas and water utilities. The companies in this sector require an extensive infrastructure and are therefore heavily indebted. If interest rates rise or fall, debt payments will rise or fall accordingly. Therefore, this sector generally performs best when interest rates are low.

In this sector, Edison International (3.77%) and The Southern Company (3.71%) are good dividend payers.

PART 3: HOW DO I PREPARE FOR INCOME INVESTMENT?

1. How much should I save?

The amount you can save from your income (after taxes) is your *savings rate*. Many income investors save a certain percentage of their income every month. This rate ultimately determines how long it will take you to become financially free, or to achieve financial independence. The financial industry generally recommends a savings rate of 10% of your income. I do not think that this is good advice. For most people, it means that their savings rate will be somewhere between USD 150 and USD 300, depending on their income.

While such a savings rate is better than nothing, it is still too low to become financially free within ten or even twenty years, even with a dividend strategy.

The examples in Chapter 4 will illustrate this. First, the regularity of your savings rate is important. You should do everything possible not to break the chain of monthly contributions to your investment account. On the other hand, the level of your savings rate also plays a decisive role. The more you can invest each month, the faster the compound interest effect will work in your favor. So, look at the examples in order to get an estimate of how much you need to save to reach your goal.

I can tell you one thing in advance. Once you start saving and you can see how the monthly dividends start to come in, you will become more and more motivated. The immediate results will help you to stay disciplined and keep your savings steady. It might even motivate you to increase your savings rate.

As with all things, you will be more motivated if you see the impact of your monthly efforts for yourself. You can see with your own eyes how the shares you own in the companies are paying more and more dividends from quarter to quarter. This is very motivating indeed.

The perception of the cash flow in your stock portfolio is quite different from the motivation that you might get from the usual savings plans or life insurance policies (if they provide any motivation at all). With this form of "investing", you will, at best, receive a financial statement once a year. You get an abstract number on paper that does not really mean much to you. Moreover, enthusiasm is not inspired at all if you consider the puny interest rates.

I once had such a pension insurance paid out after a few years, because I thought it would be stupid to pay another penny into it. Needless to say, the amount I got back from the "insurance" was much less than the total amount I had paid in, over the years. The reason for this was, of course, the administrative costs that a premature sale of my shares would entail (i.e. fat salaries for the managers of the insurance company). No wonder that the bank employee, who had sold me this "product" a few years earlier, strongly advised me not to sell prematurely.

2. How do I set up a watch list?

Perhaps you have already given some thought to which companies or sectors you would like to invest in. Maybe you have already made some notes and memorized one or more names of potential candidates. Congratulations! You have taken the first step towards building a *watch list*. Every investor who takes a somewhat systematic approach, has a watch list.

As the name suggests, a watch list is a list of stocks that you will be observing regularly from now on. The list forms the pool from which you will choose your buying candidates. This does not mean that you should buy all the shares on your list right away. Your watch list is there so that you can follow the stocks in which you currently have *no* position. Perhaps you have not bought, because the stock seems to be too expensive for you at the moment. Alternatively, maybe you have not bought yet because you do not have the money now and because you are investing your available capital in other stocks. This does not mean that it will not be possible for you to buy the stocks in the near or distant future, should a good opportunity arise. That is exactly why you have a watch list, so that you can look at the stocks that interest you every now and then.

There is no reason to rush into putting together a watch list, as if you might miss the best opportunities in the world if you did not complete your list today. On the contrary. You should rather build your list gradually, just as you should build your stock portfolio gradually. Every now and then, you will add a candidate to your list, which you think might offer a good deal some time in the future. Of course, you can also remove a stock from your list if it no longer suits your criteria.

When we come to the *selection criteria* that are important to me, I have tried to make things as clear and simple as possible. I have formulated *four questions* that I always ask myself before I put a stock on the list. Those four questions represent the checklist I use to check the suitability of potential candidates. Please note that this checklist is *my* list. This list is based on the criteria I use before I buy. If your criteria are different, or if you have additional criteria, you should add them to your list of questions.

My first question is:

Is there an ethical caveat against buying this stock?

This question may surprise some people, but in my opinion, it makes no sense to invest in a company if you consider the product or service of that company reprehensible or nonsensical. Even if the company has excellent business numbers, has regularly increased its dividends for years and would, therefore, be a good candidate for investment purposes, I would still advise against buying shares in this company.

For example, I do not buy shares of companies that are in the arms industry, because I think they are nonsensical. Raytheon, for example, is an American defense company that is a reliable dividend payer. However, as it is in the arms industry, I do not buy Raytheon shares. I am well aware, however, that many Americans and non-Americans see things quite differently.

In contrast, I have no problem with tobacco stocks. I like to smoke a good cigar, now and then. Therefore, I have no reservations about shares in Altria (until 2003 Philip Morris), who produce the well-known brand Marlboro. Altria is known for paying a high dividend. Smokers are reliable customers.

Since 2018, I have had a problem with the German Bayer stock. As you might know, Bayer bought Monsanto in 2018. Monsanto produces seeds and herbicides. The company also uses biotechnology to produce genetically modified crops, and furthermore, they produce the controversial active ingredient glyphosate, among others. Reason enough for me not to have Bayer shares in my portfolio. I simply do not want to support this, even if Bayer shares would be a good buy from an investment point of view. I want to be able to sleep at night, and I do not want to build up my retirement capital by supporting such a product.

However, I can imagine that some investors would see this differently. Everyone is free to buy what he or she thinks is good, and I think everyone should be given this freedom.

The second question might also be surprising, but in my opinion, it is just as fundamental as the first.

Do I understand the business of this company?

Regarding this second question, I would like to mention the most famous investor of our time, Warren Buffet. Buffet holds significant positions in shares of Coca Cola, McDonalds and Kraft Heinz (Heinz tomato ketchup). You can think what you like about these companies, but there is hardly a person to whom you would have to explain what McDonalds does, or what Coca Cola or tomato ketchup is. They are everyday products that every child is aware of.

Buffet has also bought shares in Apple (his company Berkshire Hathaway has a 5.6% stake in Apple). Even though Apple is a technology company, it should be no problem to explain the products of this company to a ten-year-old child (it could well be that the ten-year-old knows more about these products than you do...).

Buffet also has shares in the three most famous credit card companies Visa, MasterCard and American Express. Nowadays, everybody has a credit card. Even the ten-year-old, by the way (at some financial institutions from the age of seven!). This "product" does not need a comprehensive explanation.

The third question I ask myself is:

Would I want to inherit shares in this company?

This question may also be unexpected, at first. If you are just starting to invest, the last thing you will probably be concerned with is whether your children will like that you have a specific share in your portfolio. However, that is exactly the question you should ask yourself.

I am going to take this thing to the next level. If you had to decide which of the following two products would still be on the market in 40 years: Tesla or Coca Cola, which one would you choose?

Well, I am sure that Coca Cola will still be around. With Tesla, I am honestly not sure.

The question also has to do with probability. The well-known author of the book "The Black Swan", Nicolas Taleb, draws our attention to the *Lindy Effect* in the sequel,, "Antifragility". Simply put, this effect explains that the probability that a product that has existed for a hundred years will still exist for the next hundred years, is much higher than is the case for a product that has only been on the market for fifteen years.

Will the iPhone still exist in a hundred years? I would not bet my life on it, to be honest. However, I can well imagine that in a hundred years' time there will still be bicycles in one form or another.

As you can see, it is actually not too difficult. In that sense, as an income investor, I would put my money on companies with a long-term business model. For example, I favor companies that specialize in providing the infrastructure to make tap water available in every household. I would rather not take a company that has just developed an app that allows you to order a taxi easily (however practical and ingenious this idea may be) into consideration.

In this sense, the question of which stocks you would choose to inherit does not seem so far-fetched. After all, in thirty years' time, you still want to profit from the dividends you have saved up so hard for, not so?

Last, but not least, the fourth and final question:

Will this company pay a dividend that is attractive enough for me?

This question, which is not the last one by mere coincidence, seems to be a no-brainer. Of course, I want an attractive dividend when I buy shares. That is why I buy them.

Without a doubt, Amazon is a great company. Unfortunately, it does not pay dividends, because the philosophy of its founder, Jeff Bezos, is to invest every dollar of profit in new business areas. Maybe that will change one day. However, as long as Amazon does not pay dividends (as of April 2020), Amazon will not be on my watch list. I think that speaks for itself.

I have already covered this topic in the chapter on "High dividends or dividend growth". Nevertheless, it is worth repeating it here. An "attractive dividend" for a twenty-year-old is definitely something different than it would be for a fifty-year-old. The more time you have available to invest, the more you should focus on *dividend yield growth*. Therefore, it makes sense for a twenty-year-old to buy shares in Facebook, which has a dividend yield of 2% today (as of March 2020). That is assuming that Facebook will significantly increase its dividend over the next ten to twenty years, and has the means to do so.

If you are already in your fifties, I would rather look for shares that pay a higher dividend. A return of 4% is the minimum you should expect, and only if the dividend yield is stable and increases regularly.

It is better to find stocks with a dividend yield of 5% or more. For somebody in his fifties, the "time" is too short to profit accordingly from the compound interest effect of a strong dividend growth. Those people have to increase another variable, and that would be either the savings rate or a higher dividend.

By an attractive dividend, I also mean that the dividends of the companies that come into consideration should have increased continuously over the last ten years (preferably also during the financial crisis in 2008). Therefore, I prefer companies with a long dividend history.

If I make an exception, you can be sure that I will thoroughly analyze the company, in an attempt to find enough reasons why I should buy the stock anyway.

3. What kind of stocks is Warren Buffett buying?

Warren Buffett has almost attained the status of a saint in the investment community. For millions of investors worldwide, what Buffett buys, or says, seems to be the measure of all things. Well, I would not go that far. Do not get me wrong. What Buffett has accomplished is unparalleled. However, that does not mean you should simply copy what Buffett buys. We can learn a lot from Buffett, though, so, we can certainly use a little help from him, in order to learn what income investing is all about.

Buffett once gave the following example for evaluating a company. Suppose you would like to buy a farm. How would you approach buying it? Would you first try to find out what someone else would pay you for it later? Or, would you be more concerned with how big the farm is, what kind of revenue you could produce per hectare, what your costs would be and what cash flow the farm would generate?

I hope you have guessed that Buffett is interested in the second question. And he applies this principle to every investment he makes, regardless of whether it is a farm or any other type of business.

Now, there are many companies on the stock market, for which it might be very difficult to figure out what cash flow they could generate for you over the next ten years. For most companies, there are simply too many unknown factors that make a reasonable valuation impossible. It should be clear that these companies will not be on Buffet's watch list, whether the company is called "Tesla" or has some other hyped-up name.

If one could describe Buffet's stock selection process, it would have to go something like this:

- From the overall spectrum of companies, filter out those for which you
- can reasonably predict the cash flow for the next ten years.
- Remove companies that are run by incompetent managers from the list.
- From the remaining group, try to determine the intrinsic value of the company.
- Buy shares in the company if you can get them at a discount of 50%.

Now, it is perfectly clear to me that this may sound "simple", but in reality, it is not something that many investors can do. How would you judge whether or not the management of a company is "competent"? Moreover, how will you be able to determine the "intrinsic" value of a company?

This is also the reason why I do not use Buffett's criteria. I am just not in a position to do so.

Nevertheless, it does make sense to look at Buffett's portfolio, because you can always learn from him. I do not recommend buying exactly what Buffett buys, as some people do. You do not have the resources that Buffett has. In addition, you certainly do not have the financial means to buy into businesses as he does.

The most crucial thing you can learn from Buffet is probably common sense in investing. Buy what you understand, and buy when you can get the shares at a decent discount. That is all there is to say about it. Buffet buys shares in the best companies in the world when they are cheap. That is exactly what you should do.

4. Why I prefer American stocks

Of course, there are excellent dividend payers in Europe, Asia and South America. If you find a stock that you like from these parts of the world, there is nothing to prevent you from having it in your portfolio. The reason I prefer North American stocks (i.e. US and Canadian stocks), is the friendly stock culture of these countries.

In the United States, equities are a natural investment for retirement and it is even encouraged by the state. The attitude towards shares is simply much friendlier in the USA than it is in Europe, for example. No wonder that, in terms of percentage, many more Americans own shares, than Germans do. In 2017, the so-called shareholder ratio in Germany was just 7.7 %. If you add the funds, you get a ratio of 15.7 %. This means that 84 % of Germans have no stocks.

I also prefer US stocks, because many of them have a much longer and more robust dividend history. Furthermore, many companies in the US are much more attractive than most European stocks, in terms of fundamentals. Politicians, whether democratic or republican, actively support the companies and do their utmost to promote them. This is something you cannot necessarily always say about politicians in Europe...

Moreover, there are simply many more dividend payers in the USA, than in Europe. There are more than enough stocks available, with which to build a differentiated portfolio.

However, there is another important reason why I choose American stocks over European stocks, for my dividend strategy. The Corona crisis has once again made this clear. In Germany, at the annual general meeting, the board of directors proposes the amount of the dividend, and it has to be approved by a simple majority. During the Coronavirus crisis, all general meetings scheduled for April or May, were cancelled. Some companies took this as an opportunity to reduce, or even suspend, the dividend. The ECB (European Central Bank) asked the banks to waive the dividends. France even banned the payment of dividends to companies that would receive some form of state support because of the Coronavirus crisis.

In the USA, the board of directors of a company approves the amount of the dividend each quarter. Even if it were to be suspended once, due to exceptional circumstances, investors could at least hope that it would be paid in the next quarter, whereas most investors in European stocks would have to wait a whole year until the next annual general meeting. This is not good news for an income investor.

Despite all the enthusiasm for US equities, one should not ignore the risks. If you hold American shares and receive dividends from them, you will of course be paid in dollars. This means that you are always exposed to a certain currency risk; your investment account is not in dollars. If the dollar is strong, you will get less euros or pounds for your US dividends and vice versa. However, in my experience, currency fluctuations balance out over time. Sometimes you benefit from the dollar and sometimes you do not.

Of course, you should not buy American stocks if you do not believe in the strength of the American economy. In my opinion, it is still the strongest in the world, no matter what some people say. China is nowhere near where the Americans are today. Should this change one day, I will have to review my focus on US stocks. Nevertheless, as long as things are looking good in the USA, I will play along.

5. Who are the dividend kings?

The dividend kings are the best of the best, in terms of dividend longevity. A dividend king is a stock whose dividend has increased for fifty or more consecutive years. This is no small feat when you consider what can happen in fifty years. These companies have survived periods of inflation and deflation. They have survived the 1987 crash, the dot-com bubble and the financial crisis. In addition, they have continued to pay their dividends in spite of it all, and have even increased them from year to year!

There are currently 30 dividend kings in the USA (as of March 2020). You will certainly find suitable candidates for your portfolio on this list. Of course, you should not blindly buy the list. Some of these companies may be overvalued. Nevertheless, I am sure that almost every income investor has some of the dividend kings in his portfolio. Therefore, the list is a good place to start building your portfolio.

There are also impressive numbers that speak for the dividend kings. An investment of USD100,000 in the S&P 500 index in 1991, would have grown to almost USD1.4 million by the end of 2017, at an average annual growth rate of 10.2%. By comparison, the same investment in the current dividend kings would have grown to about USD3.2 million, representing an annual return of 13.8%.

An annual return of 13.8% in today's interest-free environment? Yes, sir. That is reason enough to look into it, I think.

If you look at the dividend kings, you will also encounter the term *dividend aristocrats*. This is a list of stocks that have increased their dividends for 25 consecutive years or more, and are on the list of the S&P 500 index.

Well, I find 25 years just as impressive. Therefore, it makes sense to look at the list of dividend aristocrats, as well. You can find several dividend pearls here too. Not a king yet, but certainly well on the way to becoming one.

Despite all the enthusiasm for these achievements, you should not buy a king or an aristocrat on the off chance, simply because you like it. Although these shares can also have a long dividend history, this is by no means a guarantee that they will continue to do the same in the future. Every now and then, a stock flies off the list because the company suddenly finds itself unable to keep its promise.

When you do your research, you should make sure that the company has not fallen into difficulties due to a crisis, which in turn could lead to dividend cuts. Sometimes, you will have to sell a stock you have already purchased for that very reason. Although you are a long-term oriented investor, you should still keep a watchful eye on your portfolio.

6. How to open a broker account?

If you have never bought a stock before, you may feel a bit overwhelmed and not really know how to start. First, you need a broker account. This is the same as a checking account, except that it is not money, but shares that are stored.

In principle, you could open this account at your bank. However, I would advise against it because you will usually pay high fees for buying (and selling) shares there. Although a lot has happened in recent years, it seems wise to choose an *online broker*. The best thing to do is to first compare the price-performance lists of the providers. there are several specialized websites internet that have already done this for you. They are easy to google.

Unlike your bank, online brokers do not operate branches. They only exist on the internet, so to speak, but do not worry; you can usually call them if you have a question. So, online brokers usually only have one website where you can log in to get access to your portfolio.

As soon as you have opened the account with your broker and deposited the money, you are ready to go. Most brokers will allow you to access the most important financial markets. This means that you can buy stocks from all over the world with just a few clicks.

As far as the dividend is concerned, you do not need to do anything. As soon as the shares of a particular company are stored in your account, you will see that the dividend is credited to your account after the dividend date. Every time you get a dividend, your cash balance will increase.

All good online brokers have a broker's license. They all need to pass FINRA's Series 7 test, which is also referred to as the General Securities Registered Representative Exam. The Series 7 Exam covers Securities and Exchange Commission (SEC) rules and regulations (if they do business in the USA). The Securities and Exchange Commission (SEC) supervises and controls all areas of finance in the USA. It also has the task of protecting consumers with regard to all financial products and services.

The question of whether the broker has a license is important. Unfortunately, some black sheep, who try to do it without a license, keep popping up, especially on the Internet. If you want to be sure, you should check the SEC database to see whether the broker is listed. You will find them on the SEC website: https://www.sec.gov/

I would also take some time to select a suitable broker. After all, he is the gateway through which you will access the world of stocks. What's more, you will have your securities account with him. You certainly want to know that your money is safe with him.

Strictly speaking, your money is not with your broker, but at a renowned bank. The account to which you will transfer your starting capital, for the purchase of shares, is and should be separate from your broker's company assets. This account is therefore called a *segregated account*. Check whether this is actually the case with your broker.

If you do not have any experience with online brokers, it is worth looking at websites that do a "broker comparison". These websites check the brokers for security, quality of service, fee structure and minimum deposit. As far as opening an account is concerned, with many brokers you can do this 100% online. However, this is not always the case. So, inform yourself. If your broker requests the documents by post, it can take ten days before your account is active. The next step is for you to transfer your starting capital to your broker's reference account. As soon as it has arrived there, you can start investing.

There are brokers such as "interactive brokers" who, for example, require a minimum deposit of USD10,000 to open an account with them. In return, you gain access to all the world markets. Other brokers like E*TRADE or Charles Schwab, do not require a minimum deposit at all. You should pay attention to the following criteria when looking for a suitable broker for a dividend portfolio:

- Free portfolio management
- Toll-free dividend payment
- No negative deposit rate
- Trading on all US and the most important international stock exchanges
- Cost per order

The cost structure is important, especially if you have little start-up capital. The "App Broker" Robinhood, a pioneer of commission-free investing, makes it extremely suitable for new investors. This broker has no minimum investment and no maintenance fees, and no commission is charged. I assume that more commission-free brokers will come onto the market in the coming years, also in Europe, South America and Asia. They would be following a trend that has already been going on for some time in the USA. Many traditional brokers have already followed suit and are offer stock trading at zero cost.

Another exciting development in the USA, is *fractional shares*. Until now, the smallest unit you could buy as an investor was *one* share. Digitalization makes it possible for one to buy half a share or even much smaller units. "Does that make sense?" you might ask.

I think so. Let us assume you are a young student and want to buy shares in a company whose stock is trading at USD 75. If you only have USD 30 to invest, you could buy, for example, a 1/3 share of the stock. You would then invest USD 25 in that stock, even though one share is three times as expensive.

Fractional shares are also interesting for dividend reinvestment plans (DRIPs). Let us take the same example. You bought 1/3 of a share and receive your first dividend. This is currently USD 3.95. For simplicity's sake, I will leave the tax out of the calculation. Therefore, you would get 1/3 of 3.95 or USD 1.31. With a DRIP program, you decide to reinvest the dividend in the same stock, immediately. Therefore, the program buys shares for USD 1.31, or at a stock price of USD 75, this would be 1/74 of the share.

This may seem like a hair-splitting exercise to some, but in the long run it is not, if you have understood the chapter on compound interest. Especially for young people with little money, investing in dividends is very interesting now, even if they can only invest small amounts such as USD 20 a month.

Let us assume that a 15-year-old starts his investment career like this today. He manages to save USD 20 a month and invests it in dividend stocks, thanks to fractional shares. Let us assume that this amount remains constant throughout his life, so even when he starts working, he still invests just USD 20 a month. How big will his stock assets be when he reaches the age of 65?

Answer: USD 346,487. He would have saved and invested a total of USD 12,000. The interest and compound interest would amount to USD 334,487. In other words, 96.54% of his assets would have been earned through interest. For the calculation, I assumed an average annual growth of the share portfolio of 10%. This includes 7% annual growth in the S&P 500, dividends of 3% and DRIP, i.e. immediate reinvestment of dividend payments. This calculation also assumes that the investor buys every month, no matter how high or low the stock market is.

Incidentally, our brave investor's assets would already be over worth USD 1.5 million if his parents had been smart enough to begin investing this USD 20 for him every month from the day he was born, but that is just an aside. As we all know, it is your grandmother's fault that you are not rich.

As you may now realize, it is smart for young people to start to invest, at an early age even with tiny sums. Firstly, they learn to invest and they can make all the mistakes in the world with their tiny stake. The faster you make all the mistakes, the faster you will learn. Secondly, with the stories of Grace Groner, Donald Read and Anne Scheiber, I wanted to show how important the duration of the investment period is. The longer it is, the more the compound interest effect can work. There is no excuse for anyone to refrain from investing. 90% of the population cannot afford *not* to invest, anyway.

7. What is the International Securities Identification Number (ISIN)?

In order to find the share in the list of thousands of shares worldwide, it is usually sufficient to enter the so-called share code. For German stocks, the abbreviation of the Siemens share is SIE. Munich Re: MUV2. Daimler: DAI. BASF: BAS.

The International Securities Identification Number (ISIN) has become increasingly widespread internationally. It is a twelve-digit letter-number combination and is used to identify securities that are traded on the stock exchange. The ISIN of Siemens AG: DE0007236101.

In the United States, however, the ticker symbols of stocks are still in use. At some point, you will know the most important ones. Everyone in the investment community knows, for example, that AAPL stands for Apple, or MFST for Microsoft.

8. Which dividend stocks should I buy now?

There is a simple formula to get an idea of whether or not a company is a good candidate for your portfolio. You should be guided by long-term considerations rather than short-term ones. A company may pay a high dividend now but still not be a good candidate.

Dividends are paid from the company's cash flow. If, for example, the current dividend is not paid out of the company's own liquid assets at all, but from a loan, this is already a warning sign for me. Therefore, it makes sense to look at the development of a company's cash flow. It is sufficient to call up the fundamental characteristics of a company on one of the many financial pages on the Internet. You will usually find everything neatly listed there: dividend history, earnings and cash flow.

What does one do if one doesn't want to deal with the fundamentals? Some readers may be able to read a balance sheet. They have the education that enables them to interpret the available figures and make an investment decision based on them. But, the majority of investors are not able to do this and do not have the time to deal with these issues (and usually do not want to).

Moreover, let's face it; if you can only invest USD 1,000 in the shares of a company, it makes little sense, in my eyes, to study the balance sheet. Anyway, the question is whether you would be able to glean something from the figures that whole armies of analysts before you have been unable to. Do you really think you could find out anything new about Apple, McDonalds or Nestle, that the analysts at the big banks have overlooked? I do not think so.

In my opinion, it is enough to read some good analyses about the stock (and hopefully understand them, because you should only buy what you understand). You may then be able to look at and compare the opinions of some dividend bloggers, but you should not spend too much time on that.

As long as you only invest small amounts of money and your monthly savings rate is USD 100 or USD 200, you should rather spend your time and energy on how to increase your savings rate. In my opinion, this is much more important than spending whole weekends thinking about the stock in which you should invest your next USD 200.

Moreover, the choice of potential candidates is not that big. Look at the portfolios of most dividend investors.

They all invest in the same stocks. Whether it is in one of the dividend aristocrats or dividend kings, the list is not endless.

There is absolutely no reason why you should invest in a completely unknown Peruvian corporation that no one here has ever heard of. If you are at the beginning of your career as an income investor, I think it is better to stick to the Coca Colas, the McDonalds, the 3Ms and the Procter & Gambles of this world. Everyone knows that these are all companies that know what they are doing, and which have a proven dividend history. So, start with the proven candidates. Later, when you have more experience, you can add "undiscovered gems" to your portfolio.

However, I doubt whether this is necessary. Take another look at the major stock positions of Anne Scheiber and Donald Read. These people bought what they knew. In addition, they bought more and more of it with the dividends they received from these companies. This is the proven method. So, do not try to reinvent the wheel.

Should you have built up significant amounts of money in a stock one day, you will certainly be more involved with it. Income Investing is a marathon. Not a sprint. It is something you grow into over time. You are on a journey that will take years and possibly decades.

Therefore, there is no need to rush in and invest all your money on the first day.

Often, it is even better to wait a little. Some income investors may wait years before they have the chance to buy shares in a particular company. Especially in the years 2015 to 2019, when most American stocks were constantly rising, it became more and more difficult to find suitable candidates. Most good dividend payers had become so expensive that it became increasingly difficult to find suitable stocks. However, when, in the wake of the Coronavirus crisis, some of these dividend payers suddenly stood at 40 or 50 % lower, there were suddenly more opportunities than you could buy. So, remember: now, when the media are predicting the biggest crash of all times, you will find exactly the opportunities you have been waiting for for years.

9. How does the Dollar Cost Average Method work?

Dollar Cost Averaging is a popular strategy for building investment positions over time. With this method, you invest equal amounts of dollars in the market at regular intervals. This means that you will be able to buy fewer stocks when prices are high and more when prices are low.

Figure 5: Buying a stock position through dollar cost averaging

Buy		Amount	Stock price	Amount stocks bought
	1	$ 1,000	$ 100	10
	2	$ 1,000	$ 80	12
	3	$ 1,000	$ 60	16
	4	$ 1,000	$ 40	25
	5	$ 1,000	$ 20	50
Total		$ 5,000	$ 44,25	113

Look at the hypothetical example in the table above. Suppose I wanted to establish a position of USD5,000 in a particular stock. Instead of investing the entire amount at once, I buy in a "staggered" fashion. In addition, of course, the best time to buy is when the stock price decreases.

In our hypothetical case, I would have bought the first position at USD 100. Therefore, since I want to invest USD 1,000 at the first buy, I can buy ten shares. Let us assume that three months later, the stock is trading at USD 80. If I want to invest another USD 1,000, thanks to the more favorable price, I can now buy twelve shares.

I keep buying into the stock, until my position is complete. As you can see, I have been buying at different prices. Sometimes at a very high rate (USD 100), sometimes at a very low rate (USD 20). In the end, I have bought a total of 113 shares. If I had invested my USD 5,000 all at once, at a price of USD 100, I would only have 50 shares!

Now, one could argue that it would have been better to wait until the price was at USD 20. Then I could have bought 250 shares with my USD 5,000. But unfortunately, unless you have a crystal ball, you do not know when the shares will fall to USD 20.

So, since I do not have a crystal ball, I use this staggered method in my stock purchases. I am happy when the price of my stock falls, because then I can increase my position and buy more, just like in the hypothetical example above.

In fact, I have bought for less than the arithmetic mean of the five purchases. If you add the five purchases and then divide by five, you get an arithmetic mean of USD60 per share. In fact, I paid an average of only USD44.25 per share to buy my entire position. That is because I can buy more shares at lower prices, than I can at higher prices. That is the beauty of this method.

So, do not make the mistake (often out of impatience!) of investing all your money in a particular stock, all at once, just because you want it in your portfolio. Impatience is one of the greatest vices when investing. As the example clearly shows, patience truly pays off.

You should also remember that, although the price of a share may decrease, this does not mean that the amount of the dividend will also decrease. On the contrary. We have already seen that good dividend payers continue to pay their dividends, even in times of crisis and sometimes, they even increase them! The strength of this method is therefore evident. If the share price decreases, I can buy more shares, and the dividend yield is higher.

Let us assume that a company currently pays USD 3 per share in dividends. If you buy the stock at USD 100, you get a USD 3 dividend per each share you hold. Your dividend yield would be 3%. If the stock drops to USD 50 and the company continues to pay a USD 3 dividend per share, your dividend yield increases to 6%. If the price of the stock drops to as low as USD 20, you will have a dividend yield of 15%.

Therefore, instead of trying to time the market, you buy at different price levels. Another advantage of this strategy is that it gives you a disciplined method for making investments. This is especially true if you regularly save a fixed amount of money. You can buy more shares when the price is low and fewer shares when the price is high.

With the commission-free brokers, you can increase your positions at any time (even the smallest units), without having to take transaction costs into consideration. You can do this on a regular basis, for example by investing a certain amount of money every month or quarter. Alternatively, you can do this only when your stock has suddenly become much cheaper, due to exceptional circumstances.

There is no right or wrong way. As the years go by, you will find that the moment at which you bought becomes less and less important. It is much more important that you stick to it and invest regularly.

This method also takes the emotions out of the game, especially when the stock market corrects sharply. Whatever the cause, as soon as the stock market starts to stumble, fear comes into play. All of a sudden, the media starts talking about the stock market again (much less in good times, as we know). The fear and panic can spread to such an extent that some people look at the stock market like a rabbit looks at a snake. Instead of entering the market, they do nothing and miss the best opportunities.

However, if you regularly invest certain amounts of money, you will eventually feel these emotions less. I deliberately say "less." Because you will still feel them. If you have not already done so, it takes some effort to buy when the price of a share, in which you already have a position, has fallen by 30% or more. However, that is just when you should buy! It is much easier to buy into a rising market. However, that is just when you should rather keep your fingers still.

I gladly admit here that I could not do that from the beginning either. I really had to learn to buy more when stocks, in which I already had positions, were suddenly trading at a discount of 50 or 60 %. That is exactly what you should learn. In times like these, you lay the foundation for your future financial independence.

As an income investor, you profit when the shares become cheaper, as paradoxical as this may sound. Because, when the price is low, you can simply buy more shares. More shares in your portfolio means more dividends. In addition, more dividends means that you can reinvest even more dividends, which in turn means that you will receive even more dividends at some point. I hope you are beginning to understand the logic behind this. Moreover, I hope you are beginning to understand why dividend stocks are one of the best ways to build long-term wealth.

10. What is a dividend reinvestment plan (DRIP)?

A DRIP, or Dividend Reinvestment Plan, is an instrument offered primarily by North American brokers. If you activate DRIP for a particular stock in your portfolio, you will not receive your dividend payments in cash. The DRIP program automatically uses the dividends to buy additional shares of that company. For example, if you have activated DRIP for a U.S. stock, the program will buy additional shares on the record date, according the amount of the dividend payment. This usually happens four times a year.

In this way, the number of shares you own automatically increases four times a year. If the number of shares in a particular company increases, you will automatically receive more dividends. In turn, more dividends mean that the DRIP program can buy you even more shares, and so on.

I hope you see the advantage of this program. Over time, the number of shares you own will "grow" automatically. Therefore, your position in a particular stock will grow from quarter to quarter. The regular reinvestment and the time factor thus creates a significant compound interest effect. This effect is independent of the share price and happens without you having to provide additional funds to invest in this share.

In the USA, there are over 1,000 companies and funds that offer DRIP plans. However, as an investor, you can have the dividends of most companies reinvested automatically through your broker. It should be noted, however, that most European brokers do not offer DRIP plans and, if they do, they usually only offer DRIP plans for American stocks. Therefore, if you want to work with automated DRIP plans, you will usually need an American broker. So, ask your broker whether he offers DRIP before you open an account with him. DRIP plans are therefore of particular interest to investors who want the mathematics of the compound interest effect to work for them in the long term.

11. Why monthly payers are interesting

As you gradually build up a dividend portfolio, you will soon find that there are months when you receive plenty of dividends and months when your pipelines are less abundant. Of course, this has to do with the fact that most American companies are quarterly payers, so every four months they pay ¼ of the total dividend. If the focus in your portfolio is on March, June, September and December, then in February or November your dividends may look rather meagre. Fortunately, not all companies pay in the same months. This ensures a certain degree of distribution over the twelve months.

For some pensioners, who are partly or completely dependent on dividends, this is an important detail. After all, your monthly costs are also evenly spread over the twelve months. You cannot call your telephone provider and say: "Sorry, but we didn't receive any dividends in February. We will pay you next month!"

That is why experienced income investors make sure that dividend payments are reasonably spread over the months. If you have deep pockets, or if you can regularly invest large sums of money, things might be a little easier. Nevertheless, anyone who pays a little attention to the weighting can solve this problem.

One way to achieve a good monthly distribution is to invest part of the investment sum in so-called *monthly payers*. These are companies that pay a dividend *every month*. Yes, you read correctly. There is such a thing. There are even investors who specialize in exactly these monthly payers, because they want, or need, a monthly dividend.

Moreover, there are some important reasons why one should do this or why, in my opinion, it makes sense to have monthly payers in one's portfolio. Apart from the stabilizing effect of even distribution over the twelve months of the year, it is a fact that a higher frequency of payment contributes to faster growth of the portfolio.

You can reinvest the dividends faster with monthly payers, especially if you have time and are not dependent on the dividends for the time being. The more often you do this, the faster your portfolio grows. Mathematically speaking, monthly payers are fantastic.

You might think that it does not matter whether you receive a dividend of USD 3 per share once a year, or if you are paid 1/12th of that amount every month. But it does. In the long run, your assets will grow faster with a monthly dividend payer, than with a yearly or a quarterly payer. The more often you reinvest your dividends, the more time they have to multiply and grow. In the long run, for example, ten or twenty years, this makes a significant difference. After all, at some point the compound interest effect will become noticeable.

When you start out, you do not notice it. However, after six years, the monthly payer's return is already 50% higher than that of the quarterly payer. After ten years, it is twice as high. Furthermore, after another ten years, with a monthly payer you get *five times* what a quarterly payer generates. That is why monthly payers are excellent instruments, particularly for young people who have a long investment horizon in which to build up their assets effectively.

A certain amount of caution should, nevertheless, be exercised with regard to the monthly payers. One problem with monthly payers is that they often have high payout ratios. This means that the margin for possible errors is smaller, especially if the company is temporarily in financial difficulties. If you only have monthly payers in your portfolio, you run the risk that one or more of them will have to cut the dividend at some point. If the payout ratio is very high, this means that the company has little money available for future growth. As an investor, you should not forget this.

Another risk factor with monthly payers is the limited number of sectors in which they are located. Typically, you will find this type of stock among the so-called REITs (Real Estate Investment Trusts). These companies invest in real estate. Needless to say, these companies could get into trouble if another real estate crisis arose.

There is no doubt that some of these companies offer an attractive dividend yield. They can make an important contribution towards building up your assets when you get to the payout phase of your portfolio.

However, I believe it is important to point out the risks that can often be hidden, or which could be dependent on external decisions, such as interest rate hikes by central banks.

Despite all the need for differentiation, as an investor, you should primarily focus on the *quality* of the company. I, myself, try to keep a good mix of blue chips that pay quarterly and I differentiate my portfolio with selected monthly payers. In addition, I keep an eye on them. If one of them cuts the dividend, or even suspends it for a longer period, I sell the stock immediately, regardless of profit or loss. There is simply no reason for an income investor to keep shares that do not (or no longer) pay dividends, in his or her portfolio.

12. How often should I check my shares?

Even if you are an income investor with a very long investment horizon, it makes sense to check the stocks in your portfolio from time to time. If you have more than ten positions (and you might have them relatively quickly), you can quickly lose track of the stocks you hold.

You might review a stock because the situation of the company has deteriorated significantly. This does not necessarily mean that you have to sell these shares. However, you might need to keep an eye on that stock, in view of the new situation.

I usually do this four times a year. So, every quarter, I check my stocks. After all, I receive a quarterly dividend from most U.S. companies.

As you can see, the time one has to invest, in order to maintain a dividend portfolio, is quite manageable. It is by no means necessary to read ten reports on each of your shares every month. If you enjoy it, or if you are a pensioner looking for a nice occupation, there is of course nothing wrong with that.

It is by no means necessary, though. There are even times when I do not look at my portfolio for weeks, unless I want to make an additional purchase somewhere. I leave it to the power of compound interest to do its job and that is best done by leaving my portfolio alone. Just sit back and enjoy being paid month after month for having shares, which grow more and more every quarter.

You can check the growth of your dividend payments on a monthly basis. Some dividend investors keep Excel spreadsheets in which they record their monthly dividends. That way, you can watch the growth of your assets more effectively. For some people, this kind of tracking can motivate them to save even more, so that the dividends start to flow even faster. However, this by no means necessary, and even investors who only have the time to check their shares once a year can be very successful.

13. What to do if the stock market crashes?

When you talk to investors, about the topic of conversation is usually the price of the shares. Most investors are interested in buying as cheaply as possible and then selling the stock at as high a price as possible. In other words: in their eyes, good stocks are stocks that go up. Bad stocks are stocks that fall after they have been bought. The share price is what most investors are concerned about. This is important, because the share price determines whether or not they will be successful on the stock market.

By my definition, investors who focus exclusively on share prices are not investors. In my eyes, they are speculators or traders. There is nothing wrong with that. If you want to trade, you are betting that the price will rise (or fall if you are short selling). There are countless strategies that have been designed to do this successfully.

A true investor, on the other hand, is interested in *the company* whose shares he holds. Because he owns shares, he has become a co-owner of the company. In addition, income investors generally want to remain owners for a very long time. They want this, because they believe in the company. They are convinced that the company will continue to operate successfully in the future. They will mainly be concerned with the operating results. Moreover, they are naturally interested in whether the company will continue to pay a good dividend (i.e. an annually increasing dividend).

This type of investor views the stock market more like a kind of *auction*, where prices fluctuate naturally. Sometimes, stocks are cheap; sometimes, you have to pay more. Since he is the co-owner of the company, he does not intend to sell his shares, no matter how high or low the current price of his shares is.

And, if the price of the share in which he holds a position is suddenly traded at a discount of 30% or more in the "auction", this investor is more inclined to buy. "Now, they are cheap," he says to himself. "That means I can buy more shares than if they were more expensive." If he can buy more shares, the dividend payment paid by the company will increase.

In other words, income investors just love it when shares become "cheap". There is absolutely no reason to fear a stock market crash. On the contrary. Sometimes they present a perfect opportunity to go on a shopping spree.

Speculators and traders in stocks naturally fear a crash like the devil fears holy water, because they live from the price increase of their stocks. If their stocks fall, they lose money.

For the income investor, stock prices also decrease sometimes. However, they do not panic, because they want to hold them for a long time (preferably forever). They know that the price of a good company will eventually recover. Experience has shown (and studies have proven it) that, after a crash, dividend stocks recover better and faster than other stocks. Therefore, income investors do not fear a crash.

Those who have set up a regular savings plan for themselves and who, as a result, buy shares on a monthly basis, will sometimes buy at a high price and sometimes cheaply. Nobody knows what the lows or the highs of the prices will be. So, why should one worry about it? Leave this to the traders and speculators.

PART 4: ALTERNATIVES TO STOCKS

Alternatives to investing in the usual industrial companies definitely exist if you are looking for them. Here, I will list three of the most interesting possibilities for income investors. All three have different risk models. Before you invest in one of them, I recommend that you take a more comprehensive look at the sector. In the addendum, I will provide some links that provide further information.

1. What are Real Estate Investment Trusts (REITs)?

REITs are companies that manage real estate, which they usually own. Since they are listed on the stock exchange, investors can acquire shares in these REITs. In this sense, as an investor, you invest in real estate without having to own any yourself. The business model is very simple. The REIT leases space or collects the rents for the properties. They distribute the income to the shareholders as dividends. As an investor, you have the income without having to do any of the work.

As a rule, REITs offer attractive dividends, the percentages of which would be difficult to achieve if you managed the properties yourself.

Most REITs specialize in a particular sector of the property market, but some REITs manage broadly diversified portfolios, with properties in a wide range of sectors.

A distinction is made between *equity REITs*, which invest in malls, residential buildings and commercial buildings, which they then sublet, and *mortgage REITs*. Mortgage REITS do not own any real estate themselves. They give loans to property owners and can buy existing loans. These companies make money from the interest on mortgage loans that they lend to residential and commercial properties. The mortgages they issue or buy pay them a higher interest rate than the short-term interest rate they pay to finance their own business. This allows them to increase their profit margins and pay higher dividends.

There are REITs in the following sectors

- Hotels
- Apartments
- Office buildings
- Retail centers and malls
- Data centers
- Infrastructure (fiber optic cables, power lines)
- Forest areas
- Warehouses

Of course, certain conditions exist for REITS. They must invest at least 75% of their total assets in real estate, cash or American bonds. In addition, they must generate 75% of their gross income from property rents, mortgage interest to finance the property or from property sales.

Interesting for the income investor: The REIT must distribute at least 90% of its taxable income to shareholders in the form of dividends. REITs are therefore shareholder-friendly companies with attractive dividends. REITs can be an important contribution to your wealth accumulation.

What is the difference between a REIT and a closed or open-ended real estate fund?

If you want to sell your shares in these funds, the management must pay them out of the fund assets. This is usually not a problem, if you are the only one who wants to sell, and if the size of your shares is modest. But if many investors want to sell (as during the financial crisis in 2008), the fund can quickly run into liquidity problems, and must start selling valuable properties, which in turn puts additional pressure on the market. This is exactly what we experienced during the financial crisis.

If you own REITs, you can sell them on the stock market with just a few clicks. Then another investor has your shares. You have to be aware that REITs are not risk-free. During the Corona crisis, for example, shares in EPR Properties lost 80% of their market value. EPR is a company that invests in amusement parks, theatres and ski resorts. After these were all closed down during the Corona crisis, investors across the board sold their shares. However, this means that you could buy them back at very low prices.

2. What are Business Development Companies (BDCs)?

BDCs (Business Development Companies) are another group of alternative investments. These companies invest in start-ups and small or medium-sized companies. They can do this with equity, so that the BDC becomes co-owner, or alternatively, they lend money to the companies that cannot easily finance themselves through bonds or bank loans.

In this way, they fulfil a dual function. They help small businesses to grow in the early stages of their development. When companies get into difficulties, they help them to regain a solid financial base.

Since BDCs are listed on the stock exchange, any investor can buy shares in them. This gives you the opportunity to participate in the market for private business loans and venture capital, which is usually very difficult for small investors to enter.

To avoid income tax, most BDCs choose the form of a *Regulated Investment Company (RIC)*. This is particularly important for the income investor, as the consequence of this decision is that BDCs must distribute at least 90% of their taxable income to their shareholders. The result is usually high dividend yields. Some BDCs generate dividend yields in excess of 10%.

However, as always on the stock market, a high yield entails an increased risk, which should not be ignored under any circumstances. Just like some REITs, BDCs often use leverage in their business model. They borrow money themselves, to lend it to the companies in which they invest. You should keep in mind that many start-ups, or smaller companies, can get into financial difficulties more quickly than established ompanies are likely to. Therefore, you should keep a watchful eye on the interest rate policy of the US Federal Reserve (FED). If the FED raises interest rates, the business model of the BDC can cause problems.

3. What are dividend ETFs?

Most investors who are familiar with the term ETF (Exchange Traded Funds), associate it with indices like the S&P500. However, there are also ETFs that contain a basket of dividend shares. As soon as the companies pay their dividends to the funds, there are two possibilities. Either the management of the ETF can distribute the dividend to shareholders in the form of a cash payment, or it can reinvest it in the shares held by the fund.

A dividend ETF is the easiest way to invest in dividend shares. Therefore, I would recommend them to investors who have neither the time, nor the opportunity, to deal with individual companies.

Since an ETF usually invests in a wide range of dividend stocks, it also offers a certain degree of protection, in the event that one of the stocks cuts or even suspends the dividend. Dividend ETFs are therefore an excellent option for beginners who do not have the necessary capital to broadly diversify their investments themselves.

Of course, you do not get this "service" for free, so it is important to look at the fund's fee structure. In my opinion, it should not exceed 0.5% per year; otherwise, the fees will have too negative an effect on your return.

If the annual return of the fund is high (over 3.5%), I would take a closer look at the portfolio. One question you should ask yourself is whether the management's investment strategy is a little too risky here and there.

PART 5: HOW MUCH DO YOU NEED TO SAVE, IN ORDER TO REACH YOUR FINANCIAL GOAL?

In order to answer this question, you first need to formulate a goal. As is well known, very few people have a financial goal in life. Why is this so? Why is it so difficult to imagine something like: "In ten years' time, I would like to earn USD 1,000 a month from my dividends, in the form of passive income?"

Actually, it is not difficult at all. However, when it comes to finances, most people shy away from formulating a concrete goal for themselves.

In order to illustrate this, I would like to show how you could achieve this, by means of some case studies. Each of us is in a different situation. We are of different ages, have different professions with different incomes and each of us has different spending habits. In addition, everyone has a different idea of what financial resources he or she will need when they reach "retirement age". Therefore, there can be no general formula. We should look at some concrete examples, in order to get an idea of how much we need to save. As an indication, you can then use the example that best suits you.

First, we need to determine which numbers we want to use to calculate our goals. It should be clear to every reader that, with these considerations, I am trying to describe scenarios that are as realistic as possible. Everyone knows that reality is usually different. You should see the three model calculations presented here as simulations, which may turn out better or worse.

I assume the following conditions for the *accumulation phase*:

- The investor has no seed capital. He starts from zero, so to speak.
- During the accumulation phase, there are no "lucky strikes" such as inheritances, unexpected business opportunities, etc.
- Since its introduction in 1926, the average total annual return of the S&P 500 Index, including dividends, has been 9.8%. While we know that we would achieve a total annual return of 13.5% if we invested in the 100 highest-yielding stocks in the S&P 500, we still choose 9.8% as a realistic target.

As soon as the investor enters the *withdrawal phase*, we have to rethink. From now on, you will not add any fresh money to the portfolio. Therefore, the growth has to be achieved 100% through price gains and dividend payments.

The classic withdrawal rule of 4% per annum, which is based on studies by financial advisor William Bengen, states that a pensioner can continue to live for at least another 33 years until his capital is used up. If he has USD 100,000 at his disposal, he can withdraw USD 4,000 annually. If he needs USD 40,000 a year, he will need a stock portfolio of USD 1,000,000. In these calculations, the most severe market declines of the 1930s and 1970s were taken into account.

The problem with this model is that the pensioner gradually consumes his capital. After a good 30 years there is hardly anything left.

If, on the other hand, the investor invests in dividend shares, he has a steady income. Instead of consuming the capital, he uses the dividend stream to finance his living costs. In this way, he preserves the capital, which can continue to grow.

Based on the significantly higher annual return of 13.5% on dividend shares, William Bengen concluded that, when using the dividend model, investors could easily choose an annual withdrawal of 5% without the capital becoming less.

Based on these figures, we now want to examine three cases, to see how much someone needs to save, in order to achieve his financial goal.

Example 1: Anita, medical assistant, 51 years old

Anita is a medical assistant who has just turned fifty-one. Her salary is USD 35,857 a year. She knows that she will have to work until the age of 66, in order not to have to accept any deductions in her Social Security Retirement. Therefore, that is another 15 working years. The Social Security Retirement benefit will be is USD 1,413 in 2035. Although her house will be paid off by then, Anita understands that she will not be able to make any big leaps with USD 1,413. She would like to have USD 500 more per month when she retires. She thinks she will need about two thousand dollars, so that she does not have to give up travelling. Anita now decides to set up a dividend savings plan, so that she can achieve her goal of "USD 500 more per month in 15 years".

How high should Anita's savings rate be if she wants to reach her goal of "USD 500 more a month"? Mind you, from 2035 onwards, she wants to receive this extra sum *monthly*, without having to consume the available capital. The following conditions must therefore be met:

Anita has to save a capital stock that yields USD 500 per month, which means USD 6,000 per year.

Her capital stock should remain constant and she should be able to increase her USD 6,000 by 2% per year, so that she can maintain her purchasing power.

Anita has done some research on the subject of dividends and dividend growth. She understands that her 15-year savings period is not long enough to really benefit from the compound interest effect that dividend growth would bring. She decides that she would rather buy shares that generate an above-average dividend yield of at least 4%. She chooses the US market because she believes it is the market where she is most likely to achieve her goals.

Her stock portfolio is therefore expected to grow by at least 9.8% per year. She understands that until 2035, there will be some years when the stock market rises and other years when it falls. However, Anita has understood the principle of income investment, and will from now on, she will invest in dividend stocks every month, no matter how good or bad the performance of the stock market as a whole is. We are assuming that Anita will not outperform the market, but neither will she underperform it. That is why we calculate Anita's savings rate based on this 9.8% annual performance of her portfolio. How high does Anita's savings rate have to be, in order to reach her goal of "USD 500 more in 2035"?

Anita runs her figures through a savings plan calculator and then through a retirement calculator. She finds that she will reach her goal if she invests USD 340 per month from today. We will go through the calculation briefly.

Anita's savings phase lasts 15 years. After this time, she will have deposited a total of USD 61,200 into her broker account. After 15 years, her deposit will have grown to USD 134,367 thanks to the annual return of 9.8%. That is the amount she will have at her disposal in 2035. From that moment on, the withdrawal phase begins. From her broker account, she transfers USD 6,000 into her checking account annually. That is the amount she needs to finance her travels.

Her dividend shares continue to generate an annual return of 5%, even after the withdrawal of USD 6,000. After one year, Anita finds that her capital has not diminished, despite the withdrawal of USD 6,000. In fact, it has grown a little. The counter now stands at USD 134,923. After five years, the figure has grown to USD 137,438.

Anita understands that she can withdraw 2% more each year to maintain the purchasing power of her USD 500. She decides to pay out 2% more, or a total of USD 6,120, next year. Even then, her portfolio continues to grow from year to year, somewhat more slowly, but it keeps growing.

Anita has reached her goal. She has USD 6,000 more at her disposal every year, with which she can take two or three nice trips, without having to consume her capital.

Example 2: Michael, student, 22 years old

Michael is studying engineering and has two more years to go before he gets his master's degree. Michael has looked at the retirement tables and realizes that demographics are playing against him. He knows that, when he retires at 66, he will have paid into the pension fund for fewer than 45 years, because he will not start working until he is 25. He decides to do something for his retirement now. With a small part-time job, he manages to put aside USD 100 a month, which he transfers to his broker account in a disciplined manner. If demographics play *against* him, he says to himself, the duration of the accumulation phase of 45 years is playing *for* him. Thanks to his knowledge of mathematics, Michael can easily calculate the compound interest effect of an accumulation phase of 45 years.

For the sake of simplicity, we assume that Michael invests in a similar way to Anita. Michael's portfolio also grows by 9.8% per year. If we now assume that Michael will continue to pay in his USD 100 a month for the next 45 years, he will have saved USD 908,734 after 45 years. With a constant portfolio growth of

9.8%, Michael can look forward to his withdrawal phase with a calm heart. Even if he withdraws USD 3,000 per month, he still has more money in his broker account after a year, namely USD 917,196. In addition, Michael could easily add 2 % every year without having to sell even one share in his portfolio.

If Michael were to invest USD 500 instead of USD 100 as soon as he starts working, he could retire at the age of 50 and withdraw USD 2,000 from his broker account every month, without using up his capital. If he saves USD 1,000 a month, which he could do as an engineer, he could retire at the age of 44 with USD 2,000 in dividends per month.

Example 3: Matthew, Walmart retail store manager, 33 years

My third example is Matthew, married, two children and Walmart retail store manager. His salary is USD 63,555. Despite this good situation, Matthew knows that his retirement, which does not start for 33 years, will not be generous. According to current calculations, he would receive USD 2,800.

Matthew is not satisfied with that. And besides, he wants to retire earlier. He would prefer to retire at 50, so that he can devote himself entirely to his hobby of Scuba diving, for which he has already taken extensive trips to the Caribbean.

He calculates that, in addition to his small pension, he will need an extra USD 3,000 per month to reach his financial goal. After reading several stock market books, he concludes that the safest and most effective way to build up assets quickly, is through dividend stocks. In order for him to withdraw USD 3,000 per month, or USD 36,000 per year, from his capital, he needs assets of USD 750,000. How much does Matthew have to put aside each month from today forward, in order to reach his goal?

The answer is USD 1,500. If he saves USD 1,500 per month, or USD 18,000 per year, he will have saved USD 306,000 in 17 years. If we also take the 9.8% annual performance as a basis, his assets would grow to USD 754,447. With this sum, he can enter the withdrawal phase and quit his job at the age of 50. Matthew knows that he will have to subject himself and his family to strict financial discipline for 17 years. He and his wife make the decision not to build a house and to stay in the relatively cheap apartment building in which they now live. All remaining debts are paid off as quickly as possible, so that the free funds are available for investment purposes. All unnecessary expenses will be radically cut, or cancelled entirely. And, in the end, after 17 years, Matthew can actually retire. His Social Security Retirement is modest, but thanks to his dividend portfolio, he has USD 3,000 more available every month.

These three hypothetical examples are a little artificial, but not too far from reality. Of course, it is impossible to make exact calculations as to how much everyone really has to invest in order to own a certain amount of X assets at the end. The 9.8% annual growth rate is a purely statistical figure, which only represents a long-term average.

It is conceivable, that one of our three dividend investors will need several years more than originally planned at the end of his accumulation phase, due to a poor stock market performance. However, it is also conceivable that the exact opposite will be the case. It could also happen faster. Especially if one of them bought during a "bad" stock market phase, i.e. at low prices, and the stock markets start to rise sharply in the years that follow, as was the case from 2009 to 2019. In this way, a few tens of thousands of invested dollars can quickly become hundreds of thousands.

Another aspect that I have ignored here is, of course, special payments or even a possible initial capital. It is conceivable that every now and then, money will be released that was not initially planned. This could be, for example, the payment of an insurance policy. Alternatively, it could be the sale of a property or an apartment, or simply an inheritance. If you look at your own life, you will see that there are always such happy events.

However, there is one sure-fire factor that we have to reckon with in any case, and which has not been taken into account in our calculations until now: tax. We will deal with this in the last chapter.

PART 6: AND FINALLY, THE TAXMAN...

Anyone planning to invest in the long term, is well advised to consider the tax structure of his investments. After all, they are among the biggest yield-killers of all, probably bigger than all the stock market corrections that an investor will experience in the course of his investing career.

Since readers from all over the world read my books, it is quite impossible to describe the exact tax situation of each country. Besides, politicians like to turn the tax screw when they need money to keep a group of voters quiet. What applies to the taxation of dividends in your country today, could be yesterday's news tomorrow.

Nevertheless, we can make some general statements regarding the taxation of dividends, which apply to most countries.

A. For US citizens

At this moment (April 2020), qualified dividends are tax-free for individuals in the 10% and 12% tax brackets (or those earning less than USD 39,375 per year). However, for taxpayers in the 22%, 24%, 32%, and 35% tax brackets, dividends receive a 15% tax rate. For individuals whose income exceeds USD 434,500 (either the 35% or 37% tax bracket), dividends are taxed at a rate of 20%.

B. For non-US citizens

If, as a non-US citizen, you plan to fill your portfolio mainly with US stocks, you should be aware of the so-called US withholding tax. This is a tax on income from capital assets that is deducted at the place of origin or source. In the USA, the tax rate is currently 30%.

However, a so-called *double taxation agreement* (DTA) exists between most countries. This agreement exists in order to prevent being taxed twice. Therefore, if you have already paid 30% tax in the USA, you do not have to pay another 25% tax in Germany, for example.

In this agreement, it was agreed that the US withholding tax would be reduced from 30% to 15%. This is then also creditable against the final withholding tax that you have to pay in Germany or France.

In order to benefit from a reduced tax rate, you must fill out the W-8BEN form (Certificate of Foreign Status of Beneficial Owner for United States Tax Withholding and Reporting) with your broker. If your broker's custodian bank has "Qualified Intermediary" status with the US tax authorities, only the reduced rate, i.e. 15%, will be withheld.

Whatever the situation might be in your country, above a certain size of fixed assets (let us say USD 100,000 or more), I think it makes sense to think about how to optimize your investments in tax terms. One thing is certain: If you plan to keep your broker account in your *personal name*, you will find yourself in the worst possible tax position. A good part of your return goes to the state.

It is therefore better to run your investments through a corporation. If this may put some readers off, you need to look at it this way. If you are serious about your financial freedom, you should explore every conceivable (and legal) way to reach your goal faster and more effectively. As long as you are still running your finances and your retirement scheme as a private person, you are an amateur, in my eyes. Then you have not yet understood the negative effect of taxes.

As Robert Kiyosaki rightly and repeatedly emphasizes: Tax laws are not made for the small guy and the "middle class" (whatever the political parties may claim). They are made for companies. The entrepreneurs and the "rich" know something that the little people and the "middle class" do not. They understand the power of the legal form of companies, and how to make the money work for them, instead of working for money like the middle class does.

ADDENDUM: INTERESTING WEBSITES FOR INCOME INVESTORS

Dividends and stock market news in general

https://seekingalpha.com/

https://www.dividend.com/

https://www.fool.com/

Stock-screener for US Stocks

https://finviz.com/screener.ashx

Compound Interest Calculator

https://www.investor.gov/financial-tools-calculators/
calculators/compound-interest-calculator

Dividend Blogger

https://www.mrfreeat33.com/

https://www.thedividendguyblog.com/

https://www.dividend-growth-stocks.com/

https://www.tawcan.com/

https://divgro.blogspot.com/

https://www.dividendgrowthinvestor.com/

Broker Comparison Sites

https://www.stockbrokers.com/compare

https://www.fool.com/the-ascent/buying-stocks/

GLOSSARY

Accumulated Dividends: Total of all distributed dividends

Arithmetic Mean: Mean value obtained by dividing the sum of the numbers considered by their number

Blue Chip: High turnover share of a large company

Broker: Financial service provider responsible for the execution of securities orders

Broker Account: Securities account, place where an investor manages his securities

Broker License: Trading license that legitimizes a broker for his activity

Business Development Companies (BDCs): Investment company in the USA that invests in small and medium-sized enterprises

Cash Flow: Business ratio in which incoming and outgoing payments within a certain period are compared

Compound Interest Effect: Interest added to the capital and paid in the future, at the applicable interest rate, together with the capital

Consumer Goods: Goods produced and traded for private use or consumption

Cyclical Consumer Goods: Essential products such as food, beverages, medicines and hygiene products

Dividend Aristocrats: List of shares that have increased their dividend for 25 or more consecutive years and are on the list of the well-known S&P 500 index

Dividend Date: Day in the USA on which the dividend is actually paid

Dividend Discount: Discount from the stock market price in the amount of the gross dividend

Dividend ETFs: ETFs that select stocks, based on the dividends paid by companies and distributed to shareholders

Dividend Growth: Regular increase of the dividend over a certain period

Dividend King: Stock, the dividend of which has increased for fifty or more consecutive years

Dividend Reinvestment Plan (DRIP): The DRIP program automatically purchases additional shares in this company with the dividends

Dividend Yield: The ratio between the amount of the annual dividend payment of a share and its current share price

Dollar Cost Averaging: Effect of regularly investing constant amounts in securities at different prices

Double Taxation Conventions (DTAs): Convention between two countries to avoid double taxation

Deposit Insurance: Statutory protective measure intended to protect creditors of credit institutions from losing their bank balances in a banking crisis

Deposit Rate: The interest rate expressed as a percentage or the sum of credited interest that an institution charges the client

ECB: European Central Bank, located in Frankfurt am Main, Germany

Equity REIT: Investment company that owns and operates real estate and generates income from the management of its real estate holdings

Fractional Shares: Part of a share smaller than one unit

Fundamentals: Key figures of a company

International Securities Identification Number (ISIN): Twelve-digit letter-number combination that provides an identification for securities traded on the exchange

Lindy Effect: Probability that a product that has existed for a hundred years will still exist in the next hundred years

Monthly Payers: Companies that pay a dividend every month

Mortgage REIT: Investment company specializing in financing income-generating real estate by purchasing or granting mortgages and mortgage-backed securities and generating interest income on these investments

Online Broker: Broker who offers securities services exclusively online

Payout Ratio: Ratio of the total amount of dividends paid to shareholders to the net profit of the company

Real Estate Investment Trust (REIT): company that acquires, manages and sells ownership of domestic and foreign real estate

Regulated Investment Company (RIC): Investment Company that does not pay tax on its income

Savings Rate: Refers to an amount of money that an investor regularly pays into an investment

Shareholder Ratio: Proportion of shareholders in the total population

Segregated Account: Account that is managed separately from the assets of the investment company, in the name of the investor

Simple Interest: Interest calculation in which the interest is not included in the respective subsequent period, thus no compound interest effect arises

Stock Portfolio: Total of all asset transactions of an investor

Transaction Costs: Costs incurred in connection with the transaction of rights of disposal (e.g. purchase, sale and lease)

Watch List: Listing of securities about whose development an investor would like to keep up to date

Withdrawal Phase: Period during which a credit balance is gradually paid out to the investor

Withholding Tax: Name for a tax levied directly at the "source" from which the income flows

W-8BEN Form: Certification of the status of the beneficial owner for US withholding tax

OTHER BOOKS
BY HEIKIN ASHI TRADER

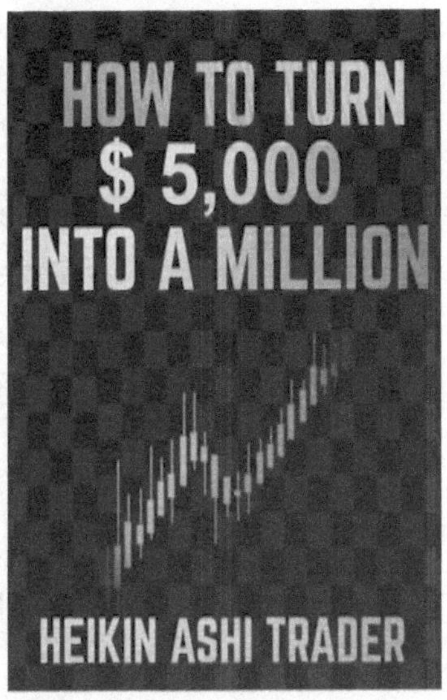

How to Turn $ 5,000 into a Million

Can you become a millionaire on the stock market? The question of how to grow a small account undoubtedly occupies every trader's mind. How do you manage to make a fortune out of a small amount? And preferably really fast?

Just as it is possible to build a real estate empire without a dollar of equity, so it is also possible to achieve high profits on the stock market with a small amount of starting capital (USD 5000 or less).

In this book, Heikin Ashi Trader presents a stock market strategy that will help the trader to succeed in this endeavor. Above all, he explains that the factor of position size plays a much more decisive role in trading success than is commonly assumed. The right question is not: how often are you right or wrong, but how big is your position if you are right?

This method is just about finding the markets where a significant movement can be expected. And once he has identified one, the trader should build a big position in that market, so that he can fully benefit from this movement.

Table of Contents

Forex Trading

The Complete Series!

As is well known, currency markets are determined by news. However, since news is rare, most currency pairs move sideways 80% of the time. In other words: it is very difficult to trade currencies profitably with trend strategies. The "Forex Trading" series therefore deals with strategies that are specifically designed for sideways markets.

Heikin Ashi Trader also discusses why traders who specialize in forex trading tend to trade only one strategy at a time. They do this because they believe it is superior to other trading methods. Unfortunately, this approach makes them vulnerable to the ups and downs of this single strategy.

However, by distributing profit and loss over several strategies, the trader creates an indifference towards the series of losses of each single strategy. If he looks at it as an investment security in his portfolio, just like a stock or a fund, he gets a more objective view on what is going on in the markets.

Part 1: Two round number strategies

Introduction

Strategy 1: The round number strategy

Strategy 2: The Stop Hunting Strategy

Consider forex trading like a probability game

Part 2: Two strategies with weekly pivots

How to trade the weekly Pivots

Strategy 1: Trade the Pivot

Strategy 2: The "last 20 Pips" Strategy

Should I change the parameters if trading is not going well?

Part 3: Trading with the Weekly High and Low

Introduction to trading with the weekly high and low

Strategy 1: Chase the Weekly High and Low

Strategy 2: Weekly High and Low Stretch

Practical questions